THE ANGER OF UNFULFILLMENT

Three Plays Out of Nigeria

JEKWU OZOEMENE

iUniverse, Inc.
Bloomington

The Anger of Unfulfillment
Three Plays Out of Nigeria

iUniverse books may be ordered through booksellers or by contacting:

iUniverse
1663 Liberty Drive
Bloomington, IN 47403
www.iuniverse.com
1-800-Authors (1-800-288-4677)

Because of the dynamic nature of the Internet, any Web addresses or links contained in this book may have changed since publication and may no longer be valid. The views expressed in this work are solely those of the author and do not necessarily reflect the views of the publisher, and the publisher hereby disclaims any responsibility for them.

Any people depicted in stock imagery provided by Thinkstock are models, and such images are being used for illustrative purposes only.

Certain stock imagery © Thinkstock.

ISBN: 978-1-4502-7488-3 (sc)
ISBN: 978-1-4502-7489-0 (dj)
ISBN: 978-1-4502-7490-6 (e)

Library of Congress Control Number: 2010918355

Printed in the United States of America

iUniverse rev. date: 12/29/2010

Chi Ejie (Night Falls)

I am! I am! The black wind howls through the cold night,
Dark cape stealthily sweeping across the murky moor,
Wet wasteland of wasted dreams dumped in a dustbin—
Dreams, dead dreams of a dead president and great beings.

Wey dem! Wey dem! the evil cyclone beckons.
No shaking! Carry go! Agbata e ke! Peter Dey Pay!
Disperse! Scatter! Drive them to the ground!
Bow or perish as the cyclone circles the money mound.

Serially sodomised, the raging tempest still raging.
Our keepers castrated, we are down on our knees praying.
Whose mother's ransom paid, whose brother's blood sprayed?
Silence! Punctuated by pin drops of muted prayers,
Wrapped in fear, who knows who are the hooded slayers?
Oh, great warriors of our land, protectors of our protectorate,
Let's all rise in unison, a call to arms on this date.
Our lone she-goat suffers the pains of parturition on its tether.
This shame is too much, this pill is extremely bitter.
Nigeria, land of great men, great minds, home for all.
Ijele dike di egwu, the dirge of a great warrior … now our song.

Silence! Punctuated by rivulets of darkness rolling in cow dung!
Chie Ejieee! Terrorists, kidnappers, criminals desecrate our land.
Freewheeling, our collective will lost in the sand.
Petrified … yes. we are, manhood, tiny little toothpicks shrivelled,
Scrotal sacs desiccated cotton balls, fire raging while we fiddle.

So, you tell me. As this pestilence decimates our land,
Are we frozen by *Agaba,* the masquerade's macabre dance?
Silence, furtive looks, shielded whispers, erectile dysfunction—
Great men now boys, toys for the marauding band.
Really? What has happened to this great land of ours?
Night falls as darkness veils half of a yellow sun.
Ijele dike di egwu, alas, the dirge that is now our swan song.
—Jekwu Ozoemene

Contents

Preface

The Anger of Unfulfillment—Three Plays Out of Nigeria is a collection of three plays: *The Anger of Unfulfillment, Hell's Invitation,* and *This Time Tomorrow.* The three plays were written and produced in the last thirteen years of Nigeria's fifty years of independence and capture a great deal of what Nigeria has come to represent today. Each play in this collection has been staged in the past and has its own distinctive flavour, seasoned by the circumstantial sociopolitical variables holding sway in the country at the time it was written.

The Anger of Unfulfillment (first staged in May 2010) examines the complex and multifaceted phenomenon of human trafficking, especially in women and girls. The play's principal characters—Adesuwa; Iyobosa; Ben; Orji; General Tinker-Tailor, a suave Niger-Delta militant; the ubiquitous Narrator; the Italian madame, Madam Boys-Quarters; and the controversial and licentious Prophet—take us through a serious but often satirical roller-coaster discourse on the Nigerian state. The discourse touches on many topical subthemes, such as militancy in Nigeria's Niger-Delta region, exam malpractice, Nigerians' love for foreign football, materialism, bribery and corruption, cultism, the scourge of kidnapping, sexual promiscuity, fraud, violence, certificate racketeering, our human development crisis, unemployment, and a host of other social vices. These vices feed the general anger in the land today, an anger we know well, fuelled by the feeling that something was promised us but never received.

The thematic preoccupation of *Hell's Invitation* (first staged in 1998) is the social death in Nigeria that is associated with HIV/AIDS. This stigma, driven by ignorance, scares Nigerians from knowing their HIV status and consequently strips them of the opportunity to seek early treatment. Through the musings and antics of Aliyu, Emeka, Stella, Bimbo, and other characters, we see and experience the social stigma through the eyes and souls of the average Nigerian.

This Time Tomorrow, on the other hand, is a comic portrait of Nigerian politicians, youth, and members of the intelligentsia/academia and their approach to politics and nation building. The play was first staged in 1999 and, through the voices of the principal characters, serves somewhat as a call to arms to the Nigerian people to take control of their destiny through active engagement and participation in national politics.

Finally, I hope that these plays will give you as much joy in reading them as they gave me in writing them, as they have become for me a comic catharsis, especially on those days when I feel that all hope for my country, Nigeria, is lost.

Jekwu Ozoemene
Port Harcourt, Nigeria
September 2010

Acknowledgments

I would like to express the deepest appreciation to my dearest wife, Pat Oghale Ozoemene, who has remained the captain of my home, juggling the intricate responsibilities of a wife, lover, mother, avid golfer, excellent dart player, and successful entrepreneur. Oftentimes I wish that God equipped me with even 50 percent of your multitasking capacity; but then, I guess that's why God gave you to me.

My prince and princess, Kaycee and Kosi—your daily early morning rumble in my bedroom remains the elixir that continually pushes me to be the best daddy that I can be, not to mention your sibling squabbles, which test my rudimentary crisis resolution and arbitration skills.

I would like to especially thank my '*besto*,' Boma Odunuga, for goading me into publishing my works; Uloma Ike for believing in me; Precious Ilobekeme Izedonmi and Isabella (Sally) Usifo for reading part of the script and giving me the 'Bini' perspective to *The Anger of Unfulfillment*; Bunmi Davies for holding the enviable record of being the only man who has directed and produced all the plays in this collection; Chioma Etuk, Bunmi Davies (again), Boma Odunuga (again), Elvis Tyronne Terrence, Adesege (Westsyde) Adeniji, and Jerry Isichei for reading the scripts and providing their invaluable critique; Tonye, my '*besto's besto*' for being there and oftentimes unwittingly catalyzing my inspiration; and Osato, Sanmi, Fatai, Emeka Ohagwu, Patrick Osadebe, Austin Edoja-Peters, Udochi Dappa, Esohe Urhoghide, Monex, Ahisu and Dapo Olagunju for always being there. Many thanks also to Dr. Olufunmilayo Adeleke, a United States-based Facebook friend, who I have never met in person but who has assumed the role of my number one fan and critic. Many thanks as well to Theatre 15 Unilag (T15) for serving as the matrix for my romance with the theatre; Tunde Euba for inadvertently introducing me to the art of directing; and Jas Hennessy & Co., bottlers and master blender of Hennessy V.S.O.P privilege cognac, a spirit that has been an able companion and muse, reigniting the fire many a night when the literary fountain appeared to run dry.

A world of thanks to my other friends as well as colleagues at Access Bank Plc, too numerous to mention here, including my exceptional and inspirational boss, Obinna Nwosu; my friends Faris and Johnny (the West-End/Haddad brothers); my friend and mentor Ichie Nnaeto Orazulike; and *Nna'm Ochie,* Sir Innocent Akuvue.

Thanks are also due to my elder brother, Uchache; my sisters, Kito, Chichi, and Nma; my darling sister-in-law, Faith, and the rest of my in-laws; my mother, Mrs. Ngozi Ozoemene (*Ifediche*); my mother-in-law, Diana Okah (Lady D); Dr. Reuben Abati, whose column in the *Guardian* newspaper of Nigeria gave life to General Tinker-Tailor and his sidekicks; and finally, my late father, Kanayo Nwuwa Ozoemene, whose life and politics partly inspired the character Professor Ogundero in *This Time Tomorrow*. It was he who guided me, albeit forcefully, into the beautiful world of books, reading, and writing.

The Anger of Unfulfillment

Characters

Adesuwa

Iyobosa

Narrator

Nari

Prophet

Madam Boy's-Quarters

Marshall

Zino

Ivie

Look-Out

Greg

Ben

Orji

Barman

Members of the congregation

A bare room with the sole furniture being a low, long altar around which are lit candles of different colours. The altar is surrounded by a circle of young men and women (dressed as if embarking on a long journey) swinging to an undulating chant led by an incense-burner-swinging Prophet. Prophet is tall, powerfully made, with an authoritative air. A stolid bald and bearded man, in his forties, he is barefoot, has no shirt on, and is sporting what appears to be a red frock over a pair of white trousers. Madam Boy's-Quarters (a plump woman in her late forties) is seen directing the proceedings. She has bleached, variegated skin, is wearing bright red lipstick, has long and multicoloured artificial fingernails, is overtly bejewelled (with rings on all fingers and nose), and has a very large hairdo and a massive backside. She bears a knowing air and seems very self-assured. There is an aura of faraway, cheap places about her.

The room is bathed in a red ominous glow, punctuated by frenzied singing and chanting from Prophet, Madam Boy's-Quarters, and the ragged congregation.

Prophet. (*Sings, accompanied by the congregation*)

> *He wrote my name with a golden pen.*
>
> *He wrote my name.*
>
> *Jesus wrote my name.*
>
> *He wrote my name with a golden pen.*
>
> *My name is there.*

(Repeated thrice, with the congregation singing in accompaniment)

Madam Boy's-Quarters. (*Whirling, almost as in an epileptic fit*) Praise the Lord! (*The now visibly charged congregation responds with a thunderous hallelujah, accompanied by clapping of hands, stamping of feet, etc.*)

Prophet. (*Sings, accompanied by the congregation*)

> *My comforter.*
>
> *Jesus is my comforter.*
>
> *Jesus is my comforter.*
>
> *I am not alone,*
>
> *Not alone.*

(Repeated thrice)

Prophet. *(Crosses himself)* Let us pray. *(Crosses himself again)* In the name of Jah.

Congregation Chorus. Amen!

Prophet. *(Looking around starry-eyed, as if searching the faces of the congregation)* Brrrrrhhhh! Zanzibar! Aaargh! In the name of Jah! Jehovah! Emmanuel! I plead the precious, incorruptible blood of Jah over you. I ask for giant warrior angels to be loosed from heaven immediately to surround and protect you.

Congregation. Amen!

Prophet. *(Moving about with energy, expressiveness)* I come against Beelzebub, the prince of darkness, his principalities, powers, and all spirit guides.

Congregation. *(Also begin to move about with energy, amidst choruses of 'Amen!' and 'Holy Ghost fire!')*

Prophet. I paralyze and silence these principals of darkness in the name of Jah!

Congregation. *(Choruses of 'Amen!' and 'Holy Ghost fire!')*

Prophet. *(Looks around starry-eyed)* Brrrrrhhhh! Aaargh! Zanzibar! *(Crosses himself)* I forbid them from strengthening local witches or wizards who want to interfere with our journey.

Congregation. *(Choruses of 'Amen!' and 'Holy Ghost fire!')*

Prophet. Oh Jah! I bind and cast them into the Kalahari Desert. Please strip them of their magic charms.

Congregation. *(Choruses of 'Amen!' and 'Holy Ghost fire!')*

Prophet. Veils.

Congregation. *(Choruses of 'Amen!' and 'Holy Ghost fire!')*

Prophet. Psychic vision and powers of divination.

Congregation. *(Choruses of 'Amen!' and 'Holy Ghost fire!')*

Prophet. *(Crosses himself)* Brrrrhhhh! Aaargh! Zanzibar! All their powers and devices will be destroyed and cast into the abyss.

Congregation. *(Choruses of 'Amen!' and 'Holy Ghost fire!')*

Prophet. *(Smiles broadly at no one in particular)* Bring them before your throne and bless them with the revelation of who you are.

Congregation. *(Choruses of 'Amen!' and 'Holy Ghost fire!')*

Prophet. *(With a deep, masculine laugh)* Then have your warriors send them back into their own bodies and seal them there with your blood!

Congregation. *(Choruses of 'Amen!' and 'Holy Ghost fire!')*

Prophet. *(Darts forward with energy)* Brrrrhhhh! Aaargh! Zanzibar! As your mighty weapon of war, I break down, undam, and blow up all walls of protection around all witches, warlocks, wizards, Satanists, and sorcerers.

Congregation. *(Choruses of 'Amen!' and 'Holy Ghost fire!')*

Prophet. *(Violently flailing his arms)* I break the power of their curses!

Congregation. *(Choruses of 'Amen!' and 'Holy Ghost fire!')*

Prophet. *(Moving about with energy, expressiveness)* Hexes!

Congregation. *(Choruses of 'Amen!' and 'Holy Ghost fire!')*

Prophet. Vexes!

Congregation. *(Choruses of 'Amen!' and 'Holy Ghost fire!')*

Prophet. Spells!

Congregation. *(Choruses of 'Amen!' and 'Holy Ghost fire!')*

Prophet. Charms!

Congregation. *(Choruses of 'Amen!' and 'Holy Ghost fire!')*

Prophet. Fetishes and psychic thoughts!

Congregation. *(Choruses of 'Amen!' and 'Holy Ghost fire!')*

Prophet. Witchcraft and voodoo!

Congregation. *(Choruses of 'Amen!' and 'Holy Ghost fire!')*

Prophet. Jinxes and bewitchments!

Congregation. *(Choruses of 'Amen!' and 'Holy Ghost fire!')*

Prophet. Psychic warfare! Prayer chains! Incense and candle burning!

Congregation. *(Choruses of 'Amen!' and 'Holy Ghost fire!')*

Prophet. Incantations and everything else being sent our way!

Congregation. *(Choruses of 'Amen!' and 'Holy Ghost fire!')*

Prophet. *(Whirling)* Holy Ghost fire will burn them! *(After a pause)* And return them to the sender, sevenfold!

Congregation. Amen!

Prophet. And I bind it to them by the blood of Jah!

Congregation. Amen!

Prophet. In Jah's name, I cut and burn all ungodly silver cords and lay lines.

Congregation. Amen!

Prophet. *(Hopping from foot to foot)* Holy Ghost fire! Satan, I paralyze you right now! You will not be able to use these souls any longer.

Congregation. *(Choruses of 'Amen!' and 'Holy Ghost fire!')*

Prophet. *(Turning on the congregation in an uncontrolled outburst)* Satan, I silence you in the name of Jah. You will not interfere with these souls, and they will have their own free will to make up their own minds if they want to travel to Europe.

Congregation. Amen!

Prophet. In Jah's name, I pray.

Congregation. Amen!

Prophet. *(With a beatific smile)* Please repeat after me: As one who is covered by the blood of Jah ...

Congregation. *(They repeat after him in a raucous, discordant tone.)* As one who is covered by the blood of Jah ...

Prophet. *(Moves around, touching each member of the congregation as he glides past)* I here and now reject and disown all the sins ...

Congregation. I here and now reject and disown all the sins ...

Prophet. Pacts, dedications, curses, and occult selections of my ancestors or any relatives ...

Congregation. Pacts, dedications, curses, and occult selections of my ancestors or any relatives ...

Prophet. That have been passed on to me intentionally or unintentionally.

Congregation. That have been passed on to me intentionally or unintentionally.

Prophet. I ask to be redeemed and cleansed from all evil curses ...

Congregation. I ask to be redeemed and cleansed from all evil curses ...

Prophet. Passed on to me from my parents, grandparents, great grandparents, ancestors, relatives, or any other person.

Congregation. Passed on to me from my parents, grandparents, great grandparents, ancestors, relatives, or any other person.

Prophet. I proclaim that I am a partaker of the inheritance of the saints of God.

Congregation. I proclaim that I am a partaker of the inheritance of the saints of God.

Prophet. I give thanks unto you, Father, for delivering me from all the powers of darkness.

Congregation. I give thanks unto you, Father, for delivering me from all the powers of darkness.

Prophet. I declare that all these curses, dedications, or pacts are null and void, in Jah's name.

Congregation. I declare that all these curses, dedications, or pacts are null and void, in Jah's name.

Prophet. I reject every way in which Satan may claim ownership of me …

Congregation. I reject every way in which Satan may claim ownership of me …

Prophet. And I command all these connected and related spirits to leave me now and never return.

Congregation. And I command all these connected and related spirits to leave me now and never return.

Prophet. In Jah's name, we pray.

Congregation. Amen!

Prophet. *(Slight pause)* Madam Boy's-Quarters, please lead us in a prayer for journey mercies.

Madam Boy's-Quarters. *(Thundering)* Praise the Lord!

Congregation. Hallelujah!

Madam Boy's-Quarters. *(Waving at the congregation with one hand, very carefully, deliberately adjusting her head tie with the other, and swinging her backside as she approaches the altar)* Praaaaaaaaise the Lord!

Congregation. Hallelujah!

Madam Boy's-Quarters. *(Moving about with energy),* Osanobua! Baba! The almighty and everlasting *Baba. We taink you ohh!* King of kings and Lord of lords. *We dey taink you ohh!* God of all creation, *na our tine be this!*

Congregation. *Yes ohh!* Amen!

Madam Boy's-Quarters. *Yes ohh! Na our tine be this! (Moves around, intermittently waving her hands and touching members of the congregation)* We honour and bless your name, for you too kind, *Baba!* You too faithful, *Baba!* We thank you for the gift of life in the name of Jah.

Congregation. Amen!

Madam Boy's-Quarters. When your son David cried out to you *(slight pause) Baba! Na ya face e dey find Baba! (Another slight pause) Na so we sef de find ya face today Baba. Monkey smart, monkey smart, na because say tree near tree.* We need your help, *Baba.* We dream of you, *Baba.* We remember that all things belong to you, *Baba.* In the name of Jah, we pray!

Congregation. Amen!

Madam Boy's-Quarters. *Osanobua don hear una prayers, na why e send me* Yes ohh! Let us pray for your sponsors. *These beta travel agents, wey be say, for small, small money, chicken change, go carry una enter Europe.* Just as Joshua sent his agents into the Promised Land, *na so dem go send una enter beta place. Abeg make una clap for these wonderful people!*

(The congregation claps whole-heartedly.)

Madam Boy's-Quarters. Amen!

Congregation. Amen!

Prophet. *(Looking straight up)* Listen to their pleas, oh Lord! For they come before you in light of your promises; you will make a way when there seems to be no way. Give us the ability to create wealth, make money, more than we can ever imagine. Please have mercy on us, oh Lord! *(Crosses himself)* Madam Boy's-Quarters. *Abeg* prayer for journey mercies.

Madam Boy's-Quarters. *(Crosses herself)* In the name of Jah.

Congregation. Amen!

Madam Boy's-Quarters. *(Moving about with energy and flailing her arms) Ose Baba! God I taink you ohh!* I commit this journey into your hands, oh Lord! The lives of your children here with me, I also commit into your able care. I decree that your angels will go before them in the name of Jah!

Congregation. Amen!

Madam Boy's-Quarters. Ah! *Baba! (Pause)* Any weapon of darkness fashioned by our enemies against us will backfire in the mighty name of Jah!

Congregation. Amen!

9

Madam Boy's-Quarters. *(Slight pause)* I take authority over the road and decree journey mercies in Jesus' name.

Congregation. Amen!

Madam Boy's-Quarters. *(Enthralled)* We cover our route with the blood of Jesus. From Nigeria to Benin Republic, Togo, Burkina Faso, Mali, Niger, Libya, and finally, Spain and Italy.

Congregation. *(Break out in frenzied choruses of 'Amen!')*

Madam Boy's-Quarters. Praise the Lord!

Congregation. Hallelujah!

Madam Boy's-Quarters. *(Moving about in a frenzy) Ya pillar of fire go dey guide us for night! Na ya pillar of smoke go protect us for day!* We will conquer Seme, drive through Krake, finish Cotonou, chop for Quidah, run things for Dohi, drink tombo for Agatogbo, rest for Gadome, come and see Come, poh-poh for Grand Popo, and sleep for Hilla Condji.

Congregation. Amen!

Madam Boy's-Quarters. From Bamako to Fana to Segou to Bla to Mopti to Sevare to Douanza to Gossi, Gao, Agadez. *Yes oh! Na ya pillar of fire by night! Then ya pillar of smoke go come guide us by day!* Every stop, every city we pass through will be covered by the blood of Jah! Let Morocco and Spain be our anointing in Jah's blessed name, we pray!

Congregation. *(A thunderous 'Amen!')*

Madam Boy's-Quarters. *(Indignantly, but laughingly)* And for those that murmur: What will we do when we get there? *How we go take survive?* What skills do we have? *Abi na Ashewo work de wan make we do?* Do they want us to be prostitutes? Are they sending us to steal? *Na wetin sef? Which wan be their own? Make dem look inside holy book! Na who save Israelite spies for Jericho? Na Rahab the harlot!* Who was the ancestor of King David? It was Ruth, *the despised Moabitess.* Who saved Nigeria from the dark-goggled General with a poisoned apple, straight from the Garden of Eden? *Na* woman, specially imported from India. That's right. *No mind them joo!* Your sacrifices will free your families from poverty. In Jah's mighty name, we pray!

Congregation. *(Choruses of 'Amen!' and 'Praise the Lord!')* *(Prophet is seen laying out an array of items on the table. These include a gourd, a bottle of local gin, alligator pepper, kola nuts, and white chalk.)*

Prophet. *(Smiles broadly at no one in particular)* As an additional spiritual insurance to our supplications to Jah, we call on the spirits of our ancestors to help forestall possible arrest and repatriation from Europe.

Madam Boy's-Quarters. Ise!

Prophet. *(Crosses himself)* Brrrrhh! Aaargh! Zanzibar! *(Moving about with energy)* We also remember the kindheartedness of our sponsors who have undertaken to send you to the Promised Land. We call on our goddess Ayelala, Ayelala! The slave woman who was wrongfully killed and now takes her vengeance from the great beyond. She who cannot be perjured, as her perjurers perish within a week. *(The congregation begins to visibly cringe.)* *(Crosses himself)* Brrrrrhhh! Aaargh! Zanzibar! Ayelala! I bring these children before you, for those who partake in eating sacrifices made to the gods surely owe the gods. Bind them by their words and bring the fear of your wrath to their conscience. You that cannot be bribed! No *mago-mago*, no awaiting trial! Death! Madness and painful death to your transgressors!

Madam Boy's-Quarters. *(Moving about with energy and flailing her arms)* Ise!

Prophet. You *(pointing to a lady in the congregation)*, come forward, come here, my daughter. What is your name?

Madam Boy's-Quarters. *Na Ivie,* Your Eminence.

Prophet. Ivie. Brrrrrhhh! Aaargh! Zanzibar! What a beautiful name, my daughter. Do you know what your name means?

Ivie. It means Jewel, Your Eminence.

Madam Boy's-Quarters. *(Avidly)* Something of great value.

Prophet. *(Scrutinizes her carefully)* Yes, my dear, you may not have brought great value along at your birth, but today I decree that you have found wealth; you will bring wealth to your family, my daughter.

Congregation Chorus. Ise!

Prophet. So tell me, do you really desire to go to Europe? Do you truly want to shed the shackles of poverty and destitution?

Ivie. *(Enthusiastically)* Yes! Yes, Your Eminence.

Prophet. Kneel. *(Ivie hurriedly goes down on her knees.)* Touch this gourd to your forehead three times *(hands her a gourd from the table)*. That's right; now touch it to your chest three times.

Prophet. *(Enthralled)* Now repeat after me: I am the beneficiary of my sponsor's kindness.

Ivie. *(Gushing)* I am the beneficiary of my sponsor's kindness.

Prophet. With my own mouth and soul …

Ivie. With my own mouth and soul …

Prophet. I hereby invite the great Ayelala …

Ivie. I hereby invite the great Ayelala …

Prophet. To visit me with the most potent misfortune and death …

Ivie. To visit me with the most potent misfortune and death …

Prophet. Should I under any circumstance reveal my kindhearted sponsor's plans to the police, immigration, or any other government authority …

Ivie. Should I under any circumstance reveal my kindhearted sponsor's plans to the police, immigration, or any other government authority …

Prophet. Or should I fail to remit to the last dollar owed to my kindhearted sponsor, as soon as I begin to earn money.

Ivie. Or should I fail to remit to the last dollar owed to my kindhearted sponsor, as soon as I begin to earn money.

Prophet. To seal this pact, we need ashes of your fingernail cuttings, ashes of your pubic hair, and eyelashes.

Madam Boy's-Quarters. *(Hands over an envelope to Prophet)* Here you are, Your Eminence.

Prophet. *(Scrutinizes the contents of the envelope carefully, then bursts suddenly into a peal of raucous laughter)* A child who inherits his father's *Babariga* does not appreciate the value of the attire. *(Pacing)* A lizard may resemble a crocodile, but their bite size clearly differentiates them. As the crocodile is shy to bite, when it does bite, it is extremely shy to let go. *(Pours the contents of the envelope into the gourd. Takes Ivie's right hand and with a razor blade makes three quick incisions)*. By this blood that you spill in this gourd *(drips the blood into the gourd)*, the heat of gin and alligator pepper *(sloshes some gin into the gourd followed by alligator pepper)*, your pubic hair *(points the gourd at her pubic region)*, that guardian to your canal of procreation, fingernails *(dips her finger in the gourd)*, the forerunner of everything you touch, and your eyelashes *(points the gourd in this direction)*, that which seals and opens the portals through which you view the world. I bind you to your sponsor, till you repay every single dollar you owe. Drink from this gourd, drink! Drink!

Madam Boy's-Quarters. *(Nodding affirmatively, with a smile)* Drink!

Congregation Chorus. *Drink! Drink! Drink! (Ivie squeamishly drinks the concoction and is ushered to her seat by Madam Boy's-Quarters. Her gait suggests some form of intoxication.)*

Prophet. Well done, Ivie. I can see that the spirit is moving you already. Your father will be very proud of you. He specifically requested that I make sure you do not disappoint him, that you make him proud. You will see for yourself. Within twelve months from today, you will be able to not only buy him the car that he desires so much, but also build a modest, modern bungalow in Benin.

Congregation Chorus. Ise!

Prophet. And that is only if you want to be modest, for by then you will be able to afford a sprawling mansion, your very own white house. Complete with a beautiful garden and a playground for your children.

Congregation Chorus. Ise!

Prophet. No man can climb to a rooftop without a ladder. This is your ladder, the moment you have been waiting for. Grab the opportunity with both hands! Who else wants to be like Ivie? Who else is willing to embark on this great journey of self-discovery with us? Who? You? *(Pointing at the other men and women)* You? What of you?

Adesuwa. (*Steps forward*) I do.

Madam Boy's-Quarters. (*Clearing her throat*) Your Eminence, *this wan na bad market. She no gree give us her somethings.*

Prophet. *Her somethings?*

Madam Boy's-Quarters. *Yes.*

Prophet. (*Crosses himself*) Brrrrrrh! Aaargh! Zanzibar! *Who be dat?*

Adesuwa. (*Calmly, indignantly*) With all due respect, Your Eminence, my religion does not permit me to engage in blood rituals with my body parts.

Madam Boy's-Quarters. (*With rising agitation*) Porca Vacca! (*Pronounced POR-kah VAH-kah*) Dammit! Who told you that we engage in *bloody* rituals? This is a covenant.

Prophet. (*Calmly*) Okay, Madam Boy's-Quarters. (*Turning to Adesuwa*) What faith do you profess? Christianity, I suppose. Do you think I am not a Christian? I am a Prophet of the Living God, a shepherd of the good Lord's flock.

Adesuwa. (*Obstinately*) Running a church does not make you a Christian, just as standing in a kitchen does not make you a cook.

Madam Boy's-Quarters. (*In an uncontrolled outburst*) Merda! (*Pronounced MEHR-dah*) Shit! I said it! *You be bad market. Bring your something you no bring! Drink from the gourd you no drink! Na only you?*

Adesuwa. (*Staring at the gourd suspiciously*) That gourd contains human blood and God knows what else. No, thank you.

Prophet. (*Thundering*) Drink it now! Drink!

Madam Boy's-Quarters. (*Exploding at her*) Oya! Drink it now! Drink! (*Pushes the gourd forcibly to her lips, but Adesuwa breaks away, backing away from her*)

Congregation Chorus. *Drink! Drink! Drink!*

Lights go to Black while a follow-spotlight picks out three men (Narrator, Orji, and Ben) seated around a table downstage left in what appears to be a bar. Narrator (sporting a leather jacket, a Bluetooth earpiece, earrings, gold rings, and gold chain with a huge pendant) is in his late thirties, handsome and well built, with an air of worldliness and knowledge about him. Where possible, the interventions of the Narrator must deliberately be played in such a way as to break the naturalistic context of the rest of the play, acting as an episodic diaphragm.

Orji and Ben are also in their late thirties, typical Nigerian corporate types, holding down 5 to 9 jobs (5:00 a.m. to 9:00 p.m.) with all the attendant frustrations. In spite of their more formal clothing, they appear less self-assured than Narrator; their jackets are slung over their seats, ties are loosed, and Ben has his sleeves rolled up. They appear to be having a drink at the end of the day's work, and a waiter is observed hustling among a number of other clients in the shadows.

Ben. *(Waving his hands in the air, speech slurred, slightly inebriated)* Orji, Nwokem! Drink! Drink! *Barman abeg bring more drinks jare. With this Lekki traffic jam, we no go fit commot here for another four hours.*

Orji. *(Conspiratorially, sotto voce through slurred speech, to Barman)* If you work on the Lagos Island and commute from the mainland, you have to get up around 5:00 a.m. Can you imagine? Five o'clock in the morning to beat the traffic.

Ben. *(Patting Narrator on the back)* My friend, as if that is not bad enough, at the close of the day, you have to stay back on the Island until 9 p.m., or else you will be stuck in the same *gaddem* traffic.

Narrator. Meaning that you work 5to 9, from 5:00 a.m. to 9:00 p.m.

Orji. *(Slurred speech)* That is it. *(Glances at his wristwatch, barely making out the time)* So, since it's just 5.30 p.m. *(looks around, waves for Barman to come over)* Drinks! Let's drink and be merry!

Ben. Correct!

Orji. *(Pointing with his glass of beer)* One Star beer for Ben, one Star beer for our new friend here, who is telling us a wonderful story by-the-way, and the coldest Star beer in the house for yours truly *(patting his chest)*.

Ben. Correct!

Jekwu Ozoemene

Orji. *(Staggering over to Narrator)* O boy this your story na real wah oh! *Mba nu!* Why will a man of God engage in such an ungodly act?

Narrator. *(Taking a swig from his beer)* Search me.

Ben. *(Picking his words carefully as tipsy people are wont to do)* Look, I agree that some so-called men of God are giving the good ones a bad name; but put it this way: they are simply taking advantage of the fact that no nation prays more than Nigerians.

Orji. *(Affirmatively)* Gbam! *(Pause, suddenly unsure)* Mba, Mba, Mba. But why?

Ben. *(Patronisingly)* Orji nwokem! You mean that you don't know?

Narrator. *(Helpfully)* Apparently he doesn't.

Ben. Okay, let me tell you. Since we don't have good hospitals in this country, we have turned our pastors and the imams into medical consultants. In fact, only in Nigeria is a pastor or imam treated like a combination of a seer and a witch doctor.

Narrator. I know what you mean. When we have challenges in our business, we go to the pastor.

Orji. *(Continuing over Narrator's lines)* When we are trying for a child, we consult the pastor.

Narrator. Their work—and we pay them handsomely for it—is to pray for us and foretell what our future holds.

Ben. Correct! That's why even as a banker, I want to change my profession, *yes oh!* *(Glances around as if waiting to be challenged)* Pastoring is a profession. *Omo,* I want my share of the business.

Orji. *(Pauses as if remembering something very important, then turns to Ben)* Ben abeg no interrupt the story again. O boy, continue with the story o jare! Meanwhile, Barman, bring three more plates of goat-meat pepper soup.

Narrator. *(Enjoying the return of attention to him)* The story is a bit undulating.

Orji. *(Gleefully to Ben)* Nna my guy, what good is a story if it doesn't have its twists and turns?

Ben. Correct!

Narrator. Before we get back to the story, however, *(to no one in particular)* where is my Star? I would like to table before you a bill I intend to sponsor to the National Assembly for the amendment of the Nigerian constitution, specifically as it affects the Oaths Act.

Orji. *(Laughing unbelieving)* The Oaths Act? Why? *(Turns to Barman) Wey the pepper soup now! (To Narrator) Nna, my guy,* leave the Oaths Act alone. In fact, leave the National Assembly alone *kpa kpa.* How will they pass any laws when they are busy struggling to increase their jumbo salary? Tell me, how?

Ben. *(Knowingly, as if divulging a well-kept secret)* Do you know that our Abuja lawmakers are the highest paid in the world?

Narrator. *(Genuinely surprised)* Really?

Orji. You mean you don't know? *(To Ben) Nna my guy, oya, tell am how much dey collect last year.*

Ben. Correct! A Senator earns $1.7 million in salaries and allowances; his House of Representatives counterpart earns $1.45 million.

Narrator. No!

Orji. Yes! *Nezinu anya?* Meanwhile, their mates in rich countries like America and Britain earn $174,000 and $64,000 in the same period.

Narrator. *(Getting agitated, slightly tipsy)* The more reason for my proposal. The magic-bullet, cure-all, surefire end to corruption. Yes, my amendment proposes that all elected officials take their oaths of office at the shrines of prequalified local deities.

Orji. *Chineke God of Israel!*

Ben. *Chei!* Not on the Bible or Koran!

Narrator. Not at all! *(Warming up to the idea)* Any Nigerian politician worth his salt knows that oaths taken on the Bible or Koran will not kill defaulters with the speed or efficacy as those taken at the shrine of a potent deity.

Orji. *(Nodding) Nna* you are right, my brother. Our politicians already seal their covenants at these shrines anyway. That is why they honour pacts made amongst themselves at the expense of the electoral pacts they have with the people.

Ben. *(Pensively)* Hmmm … So, we are simply legitimizing what is already a common practise.

Orji. *(Agitatedly) Mba nu!* Not exactly. The difference is that this one will protect our interest rather than theirs.

Narrator. In case you don't know, this proposal has already proven to be very efficient. *(Stands up; Ben and Orji follow with rapt attention)* A case in point was sometime in 2005, when the Oba Market in Benin City went up in flames. As the fire raged, hoodlums in the area had a field day looting goods. Many shops not affected by the inferno were also broken into and emptied by looters.

Ben. *Naija sha!*

Narrator. After the fire, a Pentecostal pastor went on the local radio station, pleading with looters to return the stolen goods.

Orji. I'm sure the man was ignored.

Ben. *Bifor nko.*

Narrator. His plea was quickly followed by passionate appeals by the Catholic archbishop of Benin, the Anglican bishop, and the chief imam, all appealing to the looters to please respect God and return what they had stolen.

Ben. *For where?*

Barman. *(Placing the drinks on the table) Make I open am?*

Orji. *Bifor nko! Abeg open am and commot for this place! Ewu town council! No dey interrupt our gist!*

Narrator. Finally, a prominent chief in the area invited the priest of Ayelala, a goddess widely revered and feared in Benin Kingdom.

Ben. The same Ayelala?

Narrator. The very same. The chief priest of Ayelala consequently issued a public warning that anyone who had taken away goods that did not belong to them should return same immediately or face the wrath of Ayelala.

Orji. *Ewkuzina!* So, what happened?

Narrator. For seven days, the pile of returned goods at Akpakpava Road in Benin kept growing till every stolen item had been returned.

Ben. *(With a deep, masculine laugh) Oh boy na true oh!* Just think of the kind of country we will be living in if our leaders swear to defend our constitution, not on the Bible or Koran, but at the shrine of Ayelala, Ogwugwu Okija, Ogun, Oshun, Raba Agulu, Imoka, Awosunoba, Uzere, and a host of other very potent local deities.

Orji. *(Pulls his seat nearer to Narrator) Eziokwu this your story na wah! Abeg start am from the beginning joo!*

Narrator. *(Teasingly)* It is a very long story.

Ben. *(Pulls his seat nearer to Narrator)* It is not as if we are going anywhere soon. It's just 5:30 p.m., and we still have a long wait ahead of us.

Orji. *Nna* that is why Ben and I hang out here at the close of work—to sit out the traffic. This is where we discuss both local and international issues.

Ben. Over bottles of beverages.

Orji. *Gbam!* Over bottles of alcoholic beverages. *(Sudden realisation)* I have never seen you here before.

Narrator. My wife just got a job down the road. Since I close before her, I decided to wait at this bar till she closes for the day.

Ben. *(Avidly)* Welcome to the people's parliament, my brother.

Orji. Now, where were we?

Narrator. Where do I start from?

(Ben's cell phone rings.)

Orji. *Nna put that thing for silent make e no disturb us.*

Ben. The beginning, I guess.

Narrator. Okay, then. I can say that the story started with Iyobosa.

The spotlight fades out while light comes back on stage, revealing a middle-class sitting room with an overstuffed settee flanked by two equally overstuffed chairs. A centre table and a television perched on a stool make up the principal furniture in the room. The entrance door is located downstage right, while another door that leads to a bedroom is located downstage left. A third exit door is located in the middle of the backdrop. Adesuwa (pretty, self-assured, of average height, and in her early thirties) is seen with a screwdriver, fiddling with the lock to the entrance door. A gum-chewing, overdressed Iyobosa (cocky, loud, early twenties, with an anorexic Bimbo's figure) barges in, almost banging the door in Adesuwa's face.

Iyobosa. (*Raging at no one in particular*) This is it! I'm done with job hunting! (*Plunks herself into the settee*) Why can't they just give me the frigging job?

Adesuwa. (*Still rubbing her head*) Iyobosa, you almost …

Iyobosa. (*Jumping up, oblivious of Adesuwa's pain*) *Abeg no just start your own*!

Adesuwa. Start what?

Iyobosa. *You know na* (*noisily chewing her gum, storms downstage to the apron*) that I should work harder, that 'Rome was not built in a day' (*hisses*).

Adesuwa. (*Going to Iyobosa*) Far from it. Don't you think …

Iyobosa. (*Storms away from Adesuwa, who recoils*) Think? Think? (*Hisses*) How do they expect me to think? Why do I even bother to think when the job is clearly for the highest bidder?

Adesuwa. (*Plunks herself into the settee*) You attended an interview?

Iyobosa. (*Hisses*) *Bifor!* This interview *na dem dem*. It was simply staged to make the whole thing look transparent.

Adesuwa. (*Going to Iyobosa*) I take it that the interview didn't go well.

Iyobosa. Go well? *(Takes off downstage left, to the apron)* I applied for the advertised position of a receptionist. Now tell me, what has the receptionist function got to do with international affairs?

Adesuwa. International affairs?

Iyobosa. Hmm … and I told them, I said, 'I really need this job, okay? I know nothing about international affairs, but I have very good interpersonal skills'. Did they listen to me? *For wia?* Why? Because they simply wanted me to fail the interview. They set me up to fail!

Adesuwa. Why would they set you up to fail?

Iyobosa. I asked myself the same question, then I got it. *(Thrusting a finger at Adesuwa's chest)* So that they can give the job to their friends and cronies, *dem dem.*

Adesuwa. *(Amused)* Iyobosa!

Iyobosa. Or how do you explain the difficult questions they went out of their way to ask me?

Adesuwa. Please sit down. *(Dragging her to the settee)* I'm tired of chasing you around. Like what, for instance?

Iyobosa. *(Explodes off the settee, paces the room)* All right, listen to this. A Lufthansa Boeing 737 with ninety-seven Dutch passengers on board crashed on the border of Canada and the USA. If half of the wreckage fell in Canada and the other half lies in the USA, where will the survivors be buried? *(Pause)*. Now where was I supposed to start from, ehh? Where? Lufthansa is a German airline, this plane was carrying Dutch passengers, and the wreckage lay between Canada and America. *See me see matter!* How am I supposed to know where to bury the survivors?

Adesuwa. *(With infinite patience)* You don't bury survivors.

Iyobosa. *(Stopping short)* You don't?

Adesuwa. *(Very carefully, deliberately)* Survivors are supposed to be the living, not the dead. You don't bury the living, do you?

Iyobosa. *(Drops listlessly back into the seat, shakes her head)* Now you put it that way. *Na so dey for talk na!*

21

Adesuwa. It was supposed to be a test, my dear. How else do you want them to phrase the question?

Iyobosa. *(Hisses) Over sabi!* I bet that you do not know the answer to the second question.

Adesuwa. Fire on. *(She nudges Iyobosa. Iyobosa, barely noticing, gets up and moves restlessly about the room.)*

Iyobosa. A pond has one water lily. This water lily doubles every two days. If it took the water lilies thirty days to fill the pond, on what day was the pond half full? Note that I was not told the size of the pond nor the quantity of water it contained. Okay, Miss Smart-Ass, your call.

Adesuwa. *(Rising from the settee)* I am sorry to disappoint you, Iyobosa, but the question does have a rather simple answer.

Iyobosa. It does?

Adesuwa. Yes, my dear. *(Yawning).* The lake was half full on the twenty-eighth day.

Iyobosa. The twenty-eighth day? You have completely lost me.

Adesuwa. *(Patiently)* If the water lily doubles every two days and the pond was full of water lilies on day thirty, since two halves make one whole, then the pond was half full on the day the water lilies last doubled, day twenty-eight.

Iyobosa. Oh, my God! At this rate, I will never get a job.

Adesuwa. Like I have said before, my dear, you should first concentrate on passing your university admission exams.

Iyobosa. *(In exasperation)* How can I pass an exam when I compete against cheats who have the exam papers prior to the exam?

Adesuwa. Then study more aggressively. Aim for near-perfect scores, and I bet you, you will find an institution that will be willing to take you.

Iyobosa. Everybody is cheating, so why bother to study? *Abeg leave me jo!* Look at me. For three straight years, I have sat for the same exam. Three years in succession I achieved what ordinarily should be good grades, yet I have not been able to secure a place in a university.

Adesuwa. *(Indignantly)* I will not support you to pay anyone for grades.

Iyobosa. Isn't that why I am still where I am?

Adesuwa. In our days, the worst we did was 'giraffing', discreetly peeping at a classmate's answers.

Iyobosa. Really?

Adesuwa. Yes, and of course, there was also 'desktop publishing', where we sneak into the hall the night before the exam and scribble key notes on the desk that we intend to occupy for the exam.

Iyobosa. *(Bemused)* Brilliant!

Adesuwa. Not really, as it was usually easily defeated.

Iyobosa. How?

Adesuwa *(Smiles broadly, obviously reminiscing)* The examiners learnt to reshuffle the students' sitting positions.

Iyobosa. *(Laughing unbelieving)* And you never participated in this … this giraffing and desktop publishing? I know, I know … Mother Teresa.

Adesuwa. With what goes on during examinations these days, it is clear that something has definitely gone wrong with our value system.

Iyobosa. *(Sarcastically) Oh! I don hear you!* Adesuwa, people are just trying to survive. Look around you; there are no safety nets in this country. That is why the general emphasis is on materialism. Grab as much as you can today because there may be no tomorrow. *Who be fool? Ye hemen!*

Adesuwa. *Iyhen but exams Iyobosa! (Throws an arm around Iyobosa's shoulder and walks with her down to the apron)* A good education is the very foundation on which a society, a nation is built. Exams passed through giraffing and desktop publishing will only produce half-baked graduates.

Iyobosa. *(Laughs warmly)* Giraffing and desktop publishing are things of the past. These days we purchase question papers from examiners.

Adesuwa. We? Who are 'we'?

Iyobosa. *(Backs off) No vex, I meant 'they'.*

Adesuwa. I hope so!

Iyobosa. I think I should give up seeking to study law. In truth, I actually want to be a model or maybe an actress; I am quite good in *shakara,* as you well know. We don't all have to be lawyers, scientists, engineers, or even journalists.

Adesuwa. You are right. At the end of the day, it is where your heart lies that matters.

Iyobosa. *No wahala,* but for now, I may have to join them if I can't beat them.

Adesuwa. Don't worry, my dear; you have time and age on your side.

Iyobosa. That is the one thing that Madam Boy's-Quarters told me that I don't have: time.

Adesuwa. *(Scans Iyobosa's face anxiously; after a pause)* Who is Madam Boy's-Quarters? And what kind of name is that?

Iyobosa. *(Avidly) Mama-mia!* That's her favourite phrase; call her the sunny side of my today. She is based in Italy and is a scout for international modelling agencies.

Adesuwa. *(With rising apprehension)* Is she a *Madam Italo*? Where did you meet this woman?

Iyobosa. In front of a recruitment agency I visited. *(Catwalking)* Can you imagine? She approached me, *me ke* out of all the girls who came to look for jobs. She told me straightaway, 'Cavolo! *(Pronounced KAH-voh-loh)* Wow! *Omo no mose* your figure can earn you thousands of dollars if you are willing to travel abroad … *shine ya eye girl'*. Then she gave me her contact address and number.

Adesuwa. *(Now very apprehensive)* Hmm … Tell me more about this offer.

Iyobosa. *(Gushing)* The details are still sketchy, but I have till this evening to make up my mind. She also promised to arrange a meeting with a reputable travel agent who will be willing to partly sponsor my trip.

Adesuwa. *(To Iyobosa)* Come and sit down here. The more you tell me about this Madam Boy's-Quarters, the more I distrust her. Let me accompany you to this meeting.

Iyobosa. *What is ya own self?* You don't think I am capable of handling my own affairs?

Adesuwa. Far from that. I would like to ask Madam Boy's-Quarters a couple of questions myself. Until you move out of my apartment, I remain responsible for you. At least that is what your family back home in Benin believe, so let's try and keep them happy, okay?

Enter Nari, dressed casually in a T-shirt and trousers. He is a well-sculpted man in his late thirties and exudes an air of confidence that is appealing, as well as somewhat intimidating; he is obviously a man fulfilled.

Nari. My apologies. *(With a bow)* Nari Aboloa, your new neighbour. Pardon my intrusion. I was moving my stuff into the opposite apartment and couldn't but notice that your door was ajar.

Iyobosa. *(Coquettishly)* You are welcome. Please come in. My name is Iyobosa, and my cousin and landlady is Adesuwa.

Nari. *(Another bow)* A pleasure to meet you.

Adesuwa. *(A bit unsure)* Please make yourself comfortable. That apartment has been vacant for a while; in fact, someone was supposed to have taken it up two months ago.

Nari. You are right. He is a friend of mine. He got a new job that took him out of town, so he offered the place to me.

Adesuwa. That was lucky. It is pretty difficult to get an apartment in this neighbourhood.

Nari. I know. Sorry I have to leave now; but tell me, this neighbourhood must be pretty safe for you to leave your door open.

Adesuwa. The lock is faulty. I opened the door when I got home, and the key got stuck in the lock. I was trying to fix it when Iyobosa barged in.

Nari. *(Helpfully)* Let me take a look.

Iyobosa. *(Flirtatiously)* You must be good with your hands.

Nari. Well, I have a knack for these things.

Adesuwa. (*Quickly intervening*) Are you an engineer? A technician?

Nari. (*In a squat, fiddling with the lock*) Right on the mark! (*Straightening up*) I am a mechanical engineer—a poor, struggling mechanical engineer, if I may add.

Iyobosa. (*Even more flirtatiously*) Do you also have a knack for figures?

Nari. (*Slowly looks Iyobosa over*) Figures?

Adesuwa. Not that type of figure.

Nari. Oh, okay. Figures? I should think so. Engineers deal with complex figures, complex situations, physical or social.

Adesuwa. Sounds like my work. I am a freelance journalist. You may have read or heard of my online publication, the *Naked Truth*.

Nari. (*With vast affection*) Adesuwa? You are that Adesuwa? I read your expose on the criminal elements operating in the creeks of the Niger Delta.

Adesuwa. You did?

Nari. Yes. Excellent piece. (*Pulls a screwdriver out of his pocket and takes the key out of the lock*) That General Tinker-Tailor is a scary character. Though maybe a greatly misunderstood character, given the circumstances you described.

Adesuwa. (*Beaming*) Thank you. Good to know that people read my stuff.

Iyobosa. Do you always carry a screwdriver in your pocket?

Nari. Not always, but I had to work on my door earlier as well. (*To Adesuwa*) I have always wondered, how do you make money from an online publication?

Adesuwa. For now, slim advertisement revenues, given our sometimes controversial positions.

Iyobosa. Oftentimes controversial positions.

Nari. *(Gently bangs on the door and pulls at something stuck in the lock)*

Adesuwa. Okay. Oftentimes controversial positions. Only the very bold corporate organizations, family, friends, and a few die-hard loyalists advertise through our medium.

Iyobosa. *(Unabashedly insinuating herself back into the conversation)* Back to the figures, my question is, 'Which should be heavier: a metric ton of cotton or a metric ton of fabricated concrete?'

Adesuwa. That should …

Iyobosa. *(Surly and continuing over Adesuwa's lines)* The question was not meant for you. *(Turning to Nari)*

Nari. Here you are. *(Straightening up)* The lock is ancient, but it is okay for now. It will need to be replaced to avoid a reoccurrence. As for your question, Iyobosa, a metric ton is a metric ton.

Iyobosa. *(Coquettishly)* Yes, I know it is a metric ton. That is what I said.

Nari. You don't understand? They both weigh a ton.

Iyobosa. *Ooh! Small small, explain.*

Adesuwa. *(Indignantly, but laughingly)* Whether it's a ton of concrete or a ton of cotton is immaterial. The operative word is a ton, my dear. Thanks, Nari, I guess I couldn't have fixed it better. I will definitely change the lock.

Nari. *(Another bow)* It's my pleasure. I'll have to run along as I still have a lot of furniture to move in.

Iyobosa. Need a hand?

Nari. For now, no thanks. Some of my friends are coming over to lend me a hand. If I do need a hand, though, I'll let you know. *(Exits)*

Iyobosa. Why did he turn down my offer?

Adesuwa. *(Sarcastically)* And what offer would that be?

Iyobosa. *(Sharply but controlled)* What do you mean?

Adesuwa. *(Sinking into a chair and speaking accusingly)* That you are very transparent, and don't think that I didn't notice you were flirting with him, already weaving your amorous, black-widow spiderweb designs for him.

Iyobosa. What are you talking about? Was it anything I said?

Adesuwa. More like what you left unsaid.

Iyobosa. Okay, so we are mind reading now. How can you claim you know what I left unsaid? Anyway, whatever you say, he strikes me as a nice guy. If I didn't know you better, I would think you have your own, as you put it, 'amorous black-widow spiderweb designs' for him.

Adesuwa. *(Rounding on Iyobosa)* What is that supposed to mean?

Iyobosa. *(Sidestepping, keeping out of Adesuwa's way)* Just giving you back what you gave me.

Adesuwa. So long as you remember who pays the bills in this house.

Iyobosa. *(Continuing over Adesuwa's lines)* We have been over this bill-paying thing a million and one times. If you think I've become a burden to …

Adesuwa. *(Continuing over Iyobosa's lines)* You will move in with one of your fancy boyfriends, blah blah blah. Sooner or later, your flavour of the moment will dump you again and you'll be back here, very remorseful, with your tail literally between your legs.

Iyobosa. *(Her voice subdued)* Anything you say, but something tells me that our Prince Charming had more than a passing interest for someone in this room.

Adesuwa. *(Wearily)* Please don't pull any of your legendary stunts on that guy.

Iyobosa. *(Defiantly)* Why do you think that I am promiscuous?

Adesuwa. Because you are.

Iyobosa. No, I'm not!

Adesuwa. *(Sarcastically)* My dear, why do you think that as soon as a man sets eyes on you, his sexual hackles go up?

Iyobosa. Because I have an amiable personality.

Adesuwa. *(Genuinely astonished)* Amiable personality, my foot! Has it occurred to you that it has more to do with the way you carry yourself?

Iyobosa. Me?

Adesuwa. Yes, you. You exude raw, primordial, animal sexuality. *(Sarcastically)* Why don't you simply put up a neon sign outside? 'Stud wanted; bed and breakfast on the house'!

Iyobosa. *(Pouting)* It is not my fault that men fall in love with me at first sight.

Adesuwa. *(Harshly)* News flash, my dear Iyobosa. Men don't always fall in love with you at first sight; they lust after you at first sight.

Iyobosa. And this you know from …?

Adesuwa. *(Continuing over Iyobosa's lines)* Good old experience. It's still the best teacher, my dear.

Iyobosa. If you think I'm coming between you and anything, simply say so and I'll back off.

Adesuwa. What are you talking about?

Iyobosa. You know what I mean.

Adesuwa. Of course not.

Iyobosa. *(Wearily)* Then let's let sleeping dogs lie. It is almost time for my meeting with Madam Boy's-Quarters. Still wanna come?

Adesuwa. *(After a slight pause)* Sure. Let me grab my bag.

Light fades on the set. A spotlight picks out the bar downstage left. In the orchestra pit, a group of men dressed gaily in Manchester United colours are clustered around a TV set, excitedly following what appears to be an English Premiership football match. Emanating from this group are occasional ohs, ahs, curses, and swear words that follow a missed goal-scoring opportunity or a great save; these are almost immediately followed by a thunderous 'Goal'! With backslapping, dancing, etc. Behind the bar can be seen silhouettes of people dressed in football jerseys, kneeling, with Prophet leading them in some sort of prayer.

Ben. *(Standing and peering into the audience) Nna my guy, e bi like say they done score.*

Orji. *(Clearly inebriated and enthralled, staring into his glass of beer) That Iyobosa girl no bad oh!*

Narrator. She is quite a girl.

Ben. *Na my kind babe be that. Orji my guy, you know na.*

A man dressed in Manchester United paraphernalia—jersey, scarf, etc.— walks across the bar.

Ben. *(To the Man U fan) Abeg who score?*

Man U Fan. *Up Man U!*

Orji. *(At the disappearing back of the Man U fan) Nna wetin dey worry this one?*

Ben. *(Going back to his drink) Abeg leave him jo! Na today you know say Nigerians love football?*

Orji. *Ben mba nu!* Point of correction! Nigerians love foreign football.

Narrator. It's crazy. All over the country, almost every car you see, be it rickety or luxury, is adorned with the crest of a foreign football club.

Orji. *Nna* don't mind them. Instead of supporting their home teams like *Enyimba of Aba* or *Rangers FC of Enugu,* not for Nigerians anything made in Nigeria.

Ben. *O boy na true oh!* Now that you mention it, Nigerians support only the top four teams: the winners in the English Premier League, the Italian 'Seria A', the Spanish La Liga, or the German Bundesliga.

Orji. *Mumu people!* Home teams of cities that most of them have never been to and probably will never be to in their entire lifetimes.

Narrator. Can you blame them? Our media covers mostly foreign football, and our local football clubs are hardly ever given airtime.

Orji. *Local clubs kwa? Igasikwa!* Anyway, as a travel agent, I can tell you for free that it is the same way that Nigerians struggle to migrate to Europe and North America, anyplace but Nigeria.

Ben. *But o boy!* Is it not better to go and hustle in Western countries than to live in Nigeria and suffer? *Abeg leave matter!*

Narrator. I always wonder how we can talk about the 'rule of law' when at the heart of our nation's problems is a glaring lack of respect for people's right to life, a decent life.

Orji. *Eziokwu. (Gets up gingerly, walking away)* This lack of respect for people's right to a decent life cuts across regions, tribes, and tongues … every other thing, *(waving his hands in the air expansively, drunkenly)* including the laws that can be upheld in a 'rule of law'-governed environment.

Ben. *(Continuing over Orji's lines)* Where are you going?

Orji. *Nna make I go piss. (To Narrator) Abeg make you pause your story till I come back.*

Narrator. *(Pointing at the footballers in the background)* When leaders or the led are in a tight corner, they change tactics, switch players, and turn the game around. Not our leaders or our led, for we turn to pastors, *babalawos,* marabouts, and imams; we resort to prayers and voodoo.

Ben. Let's not digress too much. What happened when they saw Madam Boy's-Quarters?

Orji staggers in, zipping his fly.

Orji. *(To no one in particular) Nna I hope say I no miss anything.*

Narrator. The address that Madam Boy's-Quarters gave Iyobosa turns out to be the Tabernacle of Thunder, Prophet's Church, consulted by the high and mighty, the rich, the poor, footballers and presidents.

Choruses rise above the Narrator's lines as light fades on the bar and comes on fully on a group of people dressed in football jerseys, with Prophet leading them in some sort of prayer.

Congregation. *(Singing and clapping)*

> Only believe,
>
> Hallelujah, only believe.
>
> All things are possible, only believe,
>
> Oh oh, only believe.
>
> Hallelujah, only believe,
>
> All things are possible, only believe. *(Repeated thrice)*

Madam Boy's-Quarters is seen detaching herself from the congregation as Iyobosa and Adesuwa walk in. She quickly ushers them to plastic chairs arranged for the congregation.

Prophet. *(Crosses himself, disperses the congregation)* God be with you, my children. You will surely win this game. Go forth and be victorious. *(Enthralled)* He who is shaking a tree is shaking himself. The venom of a viper is useless against the impenetrable shell of the tortoise's back *(thrust his right fist in the air and hollers)* Mighty!

The players respond with a thunderous 'Sparrows!' then break up and depart amidst clapping of hands, back patting, etc., already in a festive mood as if their football match has been played and won.

Prophet. *(Grandly beckoning to Iyobosa and Adesuwa)* Welcome, my children. Please feel at home. Sorry for the distraction *(pointing at the departing players)*. They come to me to ensure victory over their opponents. Just one of the little services I provide to the nation *(grinning, pleased with himself)*. You see, football is the opium of the Nigerian masses. Once our teams are winning, we are happy. When they lose, we are distraught. My God-ordained job is to keep the nation happy.

Adesuwa. *(Sarcastically)* That must be a very heavy responsibility.

Prophet. *(Avidly)* I know, I know. So you can imagine what Jah goes through, watching over all of humanity.

Adesuwa. *(Coldly)* I can imagine.

Madam Boy's-Quarters. *(With vast affection)* Una welcome. *(Turning to Iyobosa)* Iyobosa, meet Prophet, his most Eminence. He is the spiritual and financial sponsor I spoke to you about. *(Sotto voce) Na who be the Sisi wey follow you?*

Iyobosa. This is Adesuwa, my cousin and friend.

Prophet. *(Smiling warmly, steering Iyobosa away from Adesuwa)* You are most welcome, my dear. You did well to come to me, for no one can clap with just one hand. Our people say that no matter how sharp a knife is, it cannot carve its own handle. Madam Boy's-Quarters has told me that you intend to travel abroad.

Iyobosa. Yes, Europe or America.

Adesuwa works up to Prophet, Iyobosa, and Madam Boy's-Quarters, forcibly insinuating herself into the conversation.

Madam Boy's-Quarters. *(Nudging Iyobosa) Porca vacca!* Dammit!

Iyobosa. What?

Madam Boy's-Quarters. Pardon my Italian. *(Whispers conspiratorially to Adesuwa) Porca vacca* is 'dammit' in *Italo.* I keep forgetting that I am not in Italy at the moment; I'm based in Italy, you know.

Adesuwa. *(Sarcastically)* You don't mean it?

Madam Boy's-Quarters. *(Beaming)* Yes, I do, my dear. Adesuwa, please address the man of God as Your Eminence.

Prophet. *(Walking Iyobosa away from Adesuwa; Madam Boy's-Quarters follows)* I don't know what Madam Boy's-Quarters has told you, but as a rule, I do not accept money until your travel papers have been delivered.

Madam Boy's-Quarters. *(Helpfully)* The air ticket fare is borne by you.

Prophet. That is right. *(Pacing like a schoolteacher)* You will pay me a five hundred thousand naira visa processing fee, which will be paid into an escrow account. I will also take care of any other expenses which, of course, you have to pay back as soon as you start working.

Adesuwa again walks up to meet them.

Madam Boy's-Quarters. *(Walking Iyobosa and Prophet away from Adesuwa and towards the apron)* The visa fee is just twenty-five thousand to fifty thousand euros, depending on your final destination. *E no cost at all.*

Adesuwa. *(In hot pursuit)* Wait a minute! Prophet, I mean, Your Eminence, Madam Boy's-Quarters didn't mention a fee to Iyobosa.

Iyobosa. *(A look of pain crosses her face.)* No, she didn't.

Madam Boy's-Quarters. *(Growing angry)* Porca vacca! How did you expect that I would mention a fee when at the time I didn't know which country you wanted to travel to? *Even at that na still chicken change compared to the money wey you go make for that side.*

Adesuwa. *(Sarcastically)* I assume we are still talking about the modelling job?

Prophet. *(Walking Iyobosa and Madam Boy's-Quarters away from Adesuwa)* Modelling, hairdressing, or a job as a waitress. By God's grace, these things can be arranged—for the right fee, of course, for the right fee.

Iyobosa. I simply can't afford the fee you charge. If I had that amount of money, I would remain in Nigeria.

Madam Boy's-Quarters. Cheaper travel packages can be arranged.

Adesuwa. *(Barging in, increasingly sceptical)* Really?

Prophet. Yes, by God's grace, the desert option.

Adesuwa. *(With wonder)* Desert option?

Iyobosa. *Wetin be that?*

Madam Boy's-Quarters. *Be there.* That is our cheapest travel package, and his Eminence only sells it to those who the Holy Spirit has directed him to help. A lot of people he has helped in this manner became '*big boys and girls*' within one year of settling in Europe, sending home cars and cash to their families in Nigeria.

Adesuwa. *(Clapping her hands)* Eh hen! Tell me more about this desert option.

Prophet. *(Encouraged)* Due to difficulties in accessing visas, we have identified new routes to Europe through the Sahara Desert via Agadez in Niger Republic to Libya, Morocco, and Spain.

Iyobosa. *(Frightened) Omo!* Is that not dangerous? Don't people die in the desert crossing?

Madam Boy's-Quarters. People die, *bifor nko?* But people also die in their beds, in air crashes, and in road accidents. *(Raising her hands to the sky)* That is why you have to place yourself at God's mercy.

Prophet. *(Moving about with energy, expressiveness)* Just as we have no say at our own birth, so also do we have no say at our death. Everything is by the grace of God, always by his abundant mercy. The same mercy that blind Bartimaeus sought and received abundantly. The same mercy that the woman of Canaan sought and received a thousandfold. The same mercy that uplifted our very own President Goodluck Jonathan twice from a mere sidekick to his present exalted position. Shower your mercy upon us, oh Lord, according to your abundant kindness!

Adesuwa. *(Barely interested in Prophet's tirade)* Okay, okay, okay. Let us assume that we are willing to take your desert option and that we manage to cross over to Spain, does your package guarantee the modelling job?

Madam Boy's-Quarters. *Merda!* (*With hurt dignity, launching into what is apparently a well-worn sales pitch*) Shit! Modelling is hotcake now in Europe, so we cannot guarantee that oh! However, that is why we also offer jobs as hairdressers, waitresses, or bartenders. Once you get there, you should be able to do what other girls do (*winks*). Nothing better than using your God-given talent. *Abi I lie?*

Iyobosa. *(Interested)* I hear that it's easier to get a job if you are a nurse.

Prophet. Not to worry. To better prepare you for the abundant opportunities, we run an evening lesson on credit card fraud, Internet fraud, ATM fraud, and identity theft. Because of its range, the 419 Advance Fee Fraud class is a standalone course. By God's grace, we have been able to convince former students who have since travelled to Europe and become successful in their fields to provide us with real case studies.

Madam Boy's-Quarters. Don't worry, we'll make sure that you have all the skills you need before you get there.

Adesuwa. *(Sarcastically)* This is becoming more interesting.

Madam Boy's-Quarters. *Mama-mia!* Yes, it is interesting. You should count yourselves lucky that his Eminence is a man of God. Other travel agents demand sex as part of the payment. Those idiots are giving our business a bad name.

Iyobosa. *(Considering it)* Is that an option?

Adesuwa. *(Rounding on Iyobosa)* Is what an option?

Iyobosa. *(Defensively)* The sex payment.

Madam Boy's-Quarters. *Cazzo!* *(Pronounced KAHTZ-soh)* No!

Prophet. *(Interested, cautiously)* Well, that can only facilitate a deferred payment structure. In that case, your visa fee will not be made upfront but paid alongside the sponsor's fee, which is deducted from earnings in Europe.

Adesuwa. *(With rising resentment; to Iyobosa)* I think we should leave now. I have heard enough. *(To Prophet and Madam Boy's-Quarters)* Thank you so much for your time.

Prophet. *(Crosses himself)* Don't mention it *oh!* God bless you, my daughter, you are always welcome.

Madam Boy's-Quarters. Our next batch of lucky applicants will leave at the end of this week. *Make you quick quick choose the way wey you wan take waka …*

Iyobosa. I think I would prefer …

Adesuwa. *(Sharply but controlled)* Never mind. Iyobosa, let us discuss this when we get home. Madam Boy's-Quarters, not to worry; we will get back to you very soon. Have a wonderful day. *(Light fades on Prophet and Madam Boy's-Quarters as Iyobosa and Adesuwa move onto the forestage.)*

Iyobosa. *(Coquettishly)* *Mama-mia!* I think he likes me.

Adesuwa. *(Slight pause)* Who likes you?

Iyobosa. His Eminence. Didn't you notice the way he was staring at me?

Adesuwa. *(Chuckling, unbelieving)* Iyobosa, are you out of your mind? Of course, he was staring at you. Every man stares at you; every man wants to sleep with you.

Iyobosa. *(Angrily)* I think you are just jealous because I was getting all the attention. Well, it is not my fault, okay? It is not my fault that people like me.

Adesuwa. *(Emphatically)* Men.

Iyobosa. What?

Adesuwa. *(Sarcastically)* Men, you know, as in male Homo sapiens, like you. Does that not tell you something?

Iyobosa. That Prophet likes me?

Adesuwa. *(In exasperation)* You think that man likes you? Can't you see what he is?

Iyobosa. What are you talking about?

Adesuwa. *(Slight pause)* I believe that Prophet and Madam Boy's-Quarters are human traffickers.

Iyobosa. *(Unbelieving, angrily) Na lie!* A man of God and a human trafficker? Are you saying this because you are jealous?

Adesuwa. *(Dumbfounded, stares at Iyobosa in amazement)* What is there to be jealous of? I clothe you, feed you, and house you.

Iyobosa. There she goes again!

Adesuwa. *(Pauses in thought)* This will actually make a good story.

Iyobosa. What?

Adesuwa. An undercover story on Madam Boy's-Quarters and her trade. Risky, but worth it.

Iyobosa. *Haba Adesuwa! Now now you wan steal my luck?*

Adesuwa. You call this luck? You must be kidding me!

Light fades to spot on the bar.

Ben. *(Refilling his glass)* E be like say that Iyobosa girl mumu well well. *(In disappointment)* I don't like her again.

Narrator. She naively thinks she is streetwise.

Orji. *(Slurred speech)* Streetwise, my foot. *Nna, if no be for Adesuwa, she for don enter real trouble.*

Narrator. *Na so.* Every year, misled by people like Madam Boy's-Quarters, thousands of Africans, mostly Nigerians, set out on a perilous journey across the desert to Libya, from where they hope to slip into Europe.

Ben. It's such a pity. I hear that women and children make up the vast majority.

Orji rises unsteadily to his feet and pauses.

Orji. *Gbam!* What do you expect? The poverty in the land makes them vulnerable to exploitation.

He begins to walks away from the table.

Narrator. Where are you going?

Orji. To the toilet.

Ben. Really? Then you are headed in the wrong direction.

Orji turns and heads towards the toilet, swaying like a palm tree in the wind, amidst laughter from Narrator and Ben.

Narrator. Are you sure you shouldn't follow him? In his state, he can drown in his own piss.

Laughter.

Narrator. That is how many of our kinsmen drown. Desperate to scurry out of the sinking ship called Nigeria, they scurry into makeshift boats that sink in the Mediterranean.

Ben. Such a pity! *(Raises his glass and calls over his shoulder)* Barman! Serve us another round. *(To Narrator)* What are they doing on the Mediterranean?

Narrator. The Mediterranean is the desert option trafficking route.

Ben. *(Confused)* Desert, sea, hello! Am I drunk or what?

Narrator. *(Moves around restlessly and unsteadily)* On the banks of the River Niger, north of Bamako, is a city called Gao, the main starting point for illegal migrants willing to risk crossing the Sahara Desert.

Orji. *(Staggering back to his chair; to no one in particular)* I hope say I no miss anything.

Narrator. *(Using different points in the bar as milestones)* The route takes the migrants across the Malian border into Algeria, then north across the Sahara until they reach Morocco. From there, they attempt their incursion into Spain, their entry point into Europe.

Ben. *But o boy! I don talk am bifor.* Is it not better to go and hustle in Europe than to live in Nigeria and suffer? *Abeg leave matter!*

Narrator. *(Continuing over Ben's lines)* But the horrendous truth is that once these girls reach Gao, the traffickers force them into prostitution to pay for their false passports and to continue their journey.

Orji. *Chei!*

Narrator. Once again, I digress. My apologies.

The spotlight fades on the bar, and action moves back to centre stage. Adesuwa opens the door to her apartment and turns on the light switch. Nari is seen lounging on a seat (facing the entrance) in the sitting room, smoking a cigarette.

Adesuwa and Iyobosa. *(Shrieking)* What are you doing here?

Nari. *(Apologetic, rising)* Sorry, I didn't mean to scare you.

Iyobosa. *(Angry, curious)* How did you get in?

Nari. *(Dangling a key, walking towards them)* I made a copy of your key. Remember the jammed lock? That was me. Needed to do that for an opportunity to copy your key.

Adesuwa and Iyobosa retreat towards the door.

Adesuwa. *(Fumbling for her cell phone)* I am calling the police.

Nari. No, you are not. *(Zino and Marshall enter through the still-open door, caging the two women. Zino is a small, hawkish man, with fierce eyes and a loud, booming voice. Marshall is a menacing, bald but bearded mountain of a man. Both are dressed in military combat fatigues).* Even if you do, their patrol cars will either be broken down, their fuel tanks could be empty, or both. Sorry state of our country, if you ask me.

Iyobosa. *(Pleading)* Please don't rape us.

Nari. *(In disdain)* Who wants to rape you?

Adesuwa. *(Cringing)* Please don't kill us.

Nari. *(Indignantly, but laughingly)* Far from it. I need you more than you know.

Iyobosa. *(In wonder)* You need us?

Nari. I need *(slight pause)* Adesuwa.

Adesuwa. Me? Why me? What do you want from me?

Nari. I believe that at this point, we need a proper and more formal introduction. *(Bows with a flourish and escorts Adesuwa to a chair. Zino and Marshall lead Iyobosa to the opposite chair.)* My name is Iyerenari Aboloa, Nari for short, better known to the world and the oppressors of my people as General Tinker-Tailor.

Adesuwa. *(Recoils, frightened)* Oh, my God!

Iyobosa. *(Clutching her chest)* Osanobua! The militant? I thought you said you are an engineer?

Nari. *(Another bow)* Of course, I am an engineer. I graduated with first-class honours in engineering from one of the foremost universities in this country.

Adesuwa. Really?

Nari. You thought that I am an uneducated dimwit from the creeks of the Niger-Delta? I sensed that from your article.

Iyobosa. *(Rising to her feet, striking a pose)* If you don't intend to kill us, what do you want from us? *(Nari stares her down.)* I mean, from Adesuwa?

Marshall. We liked the patriotism in your article, so the general decided to grant you the opportunity to hear our side of the story.

Adesuwa. *(Gradually regaining her composure)* But the government has declared an amnesty for all militants who lay down their arms.

Iyobosa. *(Continuing over Adesuwa's lines)* Backed by huge compensation packages.

Slight pause. Nari chuckles; Zino and Marshall join in till they all break into deep, uncontrolled laughter. Adesuwa and Iyobosa stare in amazement.

Adesuwa. I'm sorry, but did we say something funny?

Zino. *(Guffawing, holding his sides, tears in his eyes)* My dear, you do not pour away the water in the earthenware pot because you hear a rumble in the sky.

Marshall. The Nigerian constitution only recognizes amnesty granted to convicted criminals.

Zino. *(Patronisingly; cleaning his nails with a big, serrated bowie knife)* To the best of my knowledge, aside from Ken Saro Wiwa and the Ogoni Nine, no one has ever been convicted over militant activities in the Niger Delta.

Nari. *(Walks down to forestage, talking almost to himself)* Even if I were to accept the amnesty, after that, what? One day I will be working down a street, and a government agent puts a bullet in the back of my head? I have ordered the death of many people, government agents included. You think they will ever forgive me for that? Even as we speak, I have it on good authority that they have infiltrated my movement and that the mole could even be one of my trusted hands.

Marshall. God forbid!

Zino. *(Plunges his bowie knife into the centre of the table with a vicious thrust. Adesuwa and Iyobosa spring back in fear.)* Impossible! It is not every animal that the hunter can afford to shoot at while standing still:

Nari. That is why the hunter may fire from the safety of a treetop. *(Slight pause)* But then, I can't be concerned about a ringworm infection when leprosy is decimating my family. History has taught us that anywhere you find peace, it was achieved through a struggle. *(Pounding his chest defiantly)* I, Iyerenari Aboloa, will play my part in this struggle.

Adesuwa. *(Fearfully)* So why do you need me?

Nari. *(Fiercely)* Before the government's spin doctors change the coloration of our story, my story, the story of my people, I have decided to get it out there first. Who better to approach than my most vociferous critic?

Iyobosa. *Abeg we no wan government wahala. Adesuwa no gree.*

Zino. *(Drawing patterns in the air with his knife and without missing a beat)* Then it will be my pleasure to kill you, both of you.

Marshall. *(Continuing over Zino's lines)* We don't believe it will get to that.

Nari. *(Very carefully, deliberately)* I have taken the liberty to come along with a recorder and writing material. *(Marshall hands over the items to him, and he hands them over to Adesuwa.)* If there is any other thing you may need, Commander Zino and Commander Marshall here will be very willing to fetch them for you.

Zino. *(Fiddling with his bowie knife)* Though a cock may belong to one man, its shrill, early morning crow serves the entire village. Make yourself comfortable and listen to the general's story.

Marshall. *(Helpfully)* Let me have a list of things you want. While you are at it, kindly hand over your cell phones. *(He collects the phones and drops them into a small duffel bag).* A tiny inconvenience for the duration of this interview: no phone calls.

Adesuwa. *(Pointing towards the bathroom)* Can we use the bathroom?

Zino. Toilet breaks are allowed. Please note that we have boarded in the window in the toilet, so no need to try and escape from there.

Nari. *(Reclining in a seat and continuing over Zino's lines)* We have men watching the streets.

Zino. Don't blame us; our elders say that a child who has been previously bitten by a snake will scamper to safety at the mere sight of a millipede. You will not like the consequences if we observe any false move. I'm sure neither of you wants that to happen.

Adesuwa and Iyobosa. (*Both shake their heads vigorously.*)

Marshall. Okay. Let's get this show on the road.

Adesuwa. (*Picking up the recorder and checking it out*)

Zino. (*To Iyobosa*) It is in perfect condition.

Adesuwa. (*Starting gingerly*) This is Adesuwa of the *Naked Truth,* your favourite online publication, where the truth is bared naked. For those of you who read our expose on General Tinker-Tailor, the dreaded Niger-Delta combatant, in our quest for a balanced story, we have invited him to give us his own side of the story. (*Switches off the recorder*) How am I doing?

Marshall. (*Impressed*) Very well; carry on.

Adesuwa. (*Switching the recorder back on*) With him are (*turns to Zino*).

Zino. Commander Zino and Commander Marshall.

Adesuwa. General Tinker-Tailor, you are welcome.

Nari. (*Apparently enjoying the moment*) Thank you.

Adesuwa. (*Warming into the interview*) So, who is General Tinker-Tailor? And how did you come about that name? I have always felt that it sounds vaguely familiar.

Nari. My real name is Iyerenari Aboloa.

Adesuwa. (*Switching off the recorder*) Are you sure that you want to reveal your real name?

Marshall. (*Confidentially*) Don't worry; this is probably the last time he will go by that name.

Nari. (*Slowly rises to his feet*) Go on.

Adesuwa. (*Switching on the recorder*)

Nari. *(Enthralled, captured by a follow-spotlight, while the rest of the set is dim)* I was born Iyerenari Aboloa, Nari for short, an Ijaw of Kalabari extraction from Abalama in Rivers State of Nigeria. At birth, my grandfather named me Iyerenari, meaning 'the famous one'.

Adesuwa. And your surname?

Nari. Aboloa literarily means 'one who did not borrow'. For we lived in a self-sustaining society, never had any need to beg or grovel for what was ours by right, what we could get from our land. My people were fishermen. That was before our lands were polluted by the exploitative actions of the international oil companies.

Iyobosa. *Which kin name be Tinker-Tailor? (Full stage lights snap on, and everyone turns to Iyobosa.)*

Adesuwa. *(Switching off the recorder).* Iyobosa, I am working here. This is a formal interview.

Nari. *(Expansively)* Never mind; I will take questions from either of you.

Adesuwa. *(Reluctantly switches on the recorder)*

Nari. Tinker-Tailor was a name I picked up from the title of a John le Carré novel, *Tinker, Tailor, Soldier, Spy.* Just liked the name, not that it bears any real meaning to who I am.

Adesuwa. So, who is Iyerenari Aboloa *(struggling with the name).* Sorry; your name is a mouthful.

Nari. You can call me Nari, if you please.

Adesuwa. Who is Nari? Some say that you are a terrorist. What is your struggle about?

Nari. *(Explosively)* Nari is a freedom fighter! *(Slight pause. Calmly)* We are freedom fighters. When I completed my university education, finishing top of my class with a first-class degree in mechanical engineering, I felt unfulfilled, till I realised that my true fulfilment lies in the struggle, the emancipation of my people, the Ijaw nation.

Adesuwa. What is this struggle about?

Zino. *(Agitated)* It's a struggle for survival! To stop the systematic annihilation of our people. Only a tree will stand and do nothing when it knows it is marked for destruction.

Nari. This is our time to be heard.

Zino. *(Continuing over Nari's lines)* And we waited this long because a child who can barely grasp the hilt of a sword should not accost his father's murderer.

Marshall. Now we are ready to claim what rightfully belongs to us.

Adesuwa. Which is?

Nari. Equity and justice and due recognition of our rights as citizens— simple.

Zino. Most importantly *(slams his knife into the table, with a vicious scowl on his face)*, the right to control our crude oil resources.

Marshall. *(Continuing over Zino's lines)* And an end to oil exploration activities that destroy the Niger-Delta ecology.

Nari. *(Vehemently)* We want the crisis of poverty in the Niger Delta addressed. We want other Nigerians to respect us as equal stakeholders in Project Nigeria. *(To no one in particular)* Is that too much to ask for?

Adesuwa. So your struggle is essentially a protest against poverty in the Niger Delta?

Nari. Yes. We had to show the rest of Nigeria that we are not stupid. Chairman Mao Tse-Tsung reminded the world that 'power grows from the barrel of a gun', and the world listened. Today we have the gun; the barrel is poked up the complacent asses of our corrupt leaders. That is our power!

Marshall. They refused to listen to our dialogue; now they have been forced to dance to the boom of our guns.

Nari. The creeks are singing and chanting defiantly, and their song is the boom of a bazooka.

Iyobosa. *(Squirms in her seat and motions Adesuwa to switch off the recorder)*

Zino. *(Angrily)* What?

Iyobosa. Toilet break.

Zino. Commander Marshall, escort the young lady to the toilet.

Adesuwa. *(Pleading)* No need for that. She does not intend to escape.

Nari. *(Pulls Iyobosa up with a finger under her chin; to Adesuwa)* You trust her that much? Commander Marshall, please escort the young lady to the toilet. No need to go in with her; just stand sentry at the door. *(Marshall exits with Iyobosa.)*

Adesuwa. *(Indignantly)* You are destroying the economy. Crisis in the Niger Delta affects government revenue, as it has a direct impact on world oil prices.

Zino. *(Beaming; wiping his knife on his arm)* That's the whole idea.

Nari. Have you heard of the economic theory of creative destruction?

Adesuwa. Joseph Schumpeter?

Nari. Yes. *(Slamming his right fist into his left palm)* We need to destroy the existing structure to build a new and enduring country.

Adesuwa. *(Shaking her head)* The world will never allow it to happen.

Zino. The world is only interested in our oil and gas.

Nari. Yes, and with the West's misadventure in the Middle East, they are looking for new sources for oil. Where else is better to come than good old ex-colony Nigeria?

Enter Iyobosa and Marshall.

Adesuwa. *(Defiantly)* How do you defend brigandage and kidnapping?

Nari. *(Shaking his head)* Kidnapping for us was not driven by criminal intentions. It was a tool for our ideological struggle.

Adesuwa. *(Contemptuously)* Congratulations! Your ideological tool has been hijacked by criminals, feeding a new breed of Mafioso, the very problem you sought to solve.

Iyobosa. *(Helpfully)* Yes, congratulations. *Una well done.*

Adesuwa. *(Eyes spitting fire)* Congratulations for what?

Iyobosa. *(Befuddled)* No be you just hail them now, now, now. I just dey copy you.

Adesuwa. *(Furiously)* Iyobosa!

Iyobosa. *(Resignedly)* Okay! Okay! I don leave you for the matta. I no go talk again.

Nari. *(Bemused)* Are you two through?

Adesuwa. Sorry about that. *(Staring Nari straight in the eye)* I said that your ideological tool has been hijacked by criminals.

Marshall. That was never what we intended. Our struggle was hijacked by criminals and reactionaries. Our original targets were the foreigners stealing our oil.

Adesuwa. So, the Nigerians who were kidnapped, the children, were those unintended victims?

Nari. *(Withering, backing off)* Some, yes … unintended consequences … but the others—our rich men and their families, politicians … all are prisoners of war, simply collateral damage. To make an omelette, you have to break an egg. For an omelette the size of our struggle, you will have to break many big eggs.

Adesuwa. *(Sotto voce)* So, how many eggs have you broken? *(Plunks into the settee, in resignation)*

Zino. *(Going to Adesuwa, helpfully)* A woman only tells her husband of the men she rejected, not the lovers that warmed her bed.

Marshall. *(Obstinately)* The killings and kidnappings will only cease when the true revolutionaries regain control of the struggle.

They all start as Look-Out pokes his head through the door.

Look-Out. *(Flustered)* How much more time do you need, sir?

Nari. Another five minutes, and we are good to go. *(Look-Out exits.)*

Adesuwa. Why don't you reconsider the amnesty offer? If not, it will just be a matter of time before law enforcement smokes you out.

Slight pause. Nari chuckles; Zino and Marshall join in till they all break into deep, uncontrolled laughter. Adesuwa and Iyobosa stare in amazement.

Zino. *(Guffawing and holding his sides)* Are you kidding me? The law enforcement agencies are unprepared for our brand of warfare.

Adesuwa. *(Stubbornly)* Innocent people are paying the price.

Iyobosa. *Bifor nko.*

Adesuwa. *(Rounds on her angrily)* Iyobosa!

Iyobosa. *(Contritely)* Sorry!

Adesuwa. *(Pleading, a threat)* General, can your men gag her for the duration of this interview?

Iyobosa. *(In shock) Haba! I have said sorry now. No need for that.*

Adesuwa. *(To Nari and his men)* Please go on.

Zino. *(Waving clenched fist in the air defiantly)* So long as the people who are paying the price are Nigerians or supporters of our oppressors, he who swallows a pestle has no choice but to sleep standing.

Nari. The Nigerian police response to our campaigns has been laughable. We belong to the creeks; we were born in the creeks. We are the ones doing the smoking out, not the police.

Adesuwa. What about the Joint Military and Police Task Force? The media says that they have drawn up strategies for the final …

Marshall. *(Laughing, going right through her speech)* Ha! Ha! Ha! So they are just coming up with strategies? Where were they when we acquired surface-to-air missiles and automatic firearms? Strategising?

Nari. *(Fist in the air)* This is the only form of pressure our government understands, the only agitation that has forced them to the discussion table.

Adesuwa. What about the victims?

Zino. Which victims?

Nari. *(Heatedly, moving to forestage)* We are the real victims here. The poor fisherman who can no longer feed his family because the oil has polluted our waters; the farmer who has hung his hoe because the soil has become too acidic for planting; the children without potable water; no schools, no hospitals, no motorable roads, yet their land produces the oil that feeds a cabal in the nation—those are the real victims.

Zino. *(Helpfully, cleaning his knife)* It is an irony that the carver of beautiful mortars and pestles has been forced to pound his yam with a broken stick.

Adesuwa. *(Ignoring Zino, storming down to Nari)* That still does not make militancy a rightful means of agitation. Our constitution criminalizes kidnapping.

Nari. *(Cutting her off)* Really? How come your government negotiates with kidnappers? Your politicians are always quick to take credit for helping to secure the release of prisoners of war captured by our people.

Adesuwa. *(Almost pleading)* What if the government turns over a new leaf? What if there is good governance at all levels, genuine and sustainable development …

Nari. *(Going right through her speech, sarcastically)* What if goats learn how to fly?

Marshall. They need to start by adequately compensating our people. Then they educate our youths, rehabilitate them, and create gainful employment.

Adesuwa. You are really very angry.

Nari. Our people live in coastal areas surrounded by water, and yet they cannot get potable water to drink.

Marshall. Profit from our crude oil was used to build Abuja and develop Lagos, yet our people have no motorable roads in their communities, cannot even afford to buy the motors that will run on the elusive motorable roads, no bridges across their rivers. Yet you wonder why we are angry?

Zino. *(Helpfully)* A little bird that perches on a long rope causes an uneasy undulation for both itself and the rope on which it perches.

Adesuwa. Peaceful agitation I understand. But your struggle has since degenerated into pure anarchy.

Nari. They created anarchy first; and in a state of anarchy and pandemonium, to be law-abiding is illegal.

Adesuwa. I empathise with your struggle; but the truth be told, it has degenerated into all forms of criminality.

Marshall. Then the government should implement the recommendations of the Willinks Commission.

Adesuwa. The Willinks Commission?

Nari. Aha! *(Professorially, pacing)* I knew that this would take you by surprise. Most people don't know that our agitation did not start recently. As far back as 1951, the people of the Niger Delta had protested against the marginalisation of their region and destruction of their environment. The clamour is over fifty-nine years old, yet nothing has been done. Just one oil spill in the Gulf of Mexico, and the whole world is up in arms.

Iyobosa. *Na wa oh! (Adesuwa glares at her.) Sorry.*

Marshall. Nigeria is the sixth largest producer of oil in the world …

Zino. *(Continuing over Marshall's lines)* … and the largest oil-producing country in Africa.

Nari. Oil is our main export and the source of 95 percent of our national revenue. But where does this revenue go?

Zino. We see very little of it. Just government statistics on how they have spent our money, our stolen commonwealth.

Adesuwa. Before the discovery of oil, Nigeria was mainly an agriculture-based country.

Marshall. *(Vehemently)* So, let them return to their agriculture and leave our oil alone!

Nari. Our people are angry. Every day they are mocked by the contrast between their lives and the standard of living enjoyed by politicians and oil company executives. We are angry, very angry.

Zino. Do you know the level of poverty, unemployment, and social degradation in the creeks of the Niger Delta?

Iyobosa. *(Surly)* Hello! There is poverty and degradation in the whole of Nigeria. I am a living testimony to that.

Marshall. *(To Adesuwa)* Just ignore her.

Nari. *(Forestage, facing the audience, looking straight up, right hand on his chest as if reciting the national anthem)* Nigeria as a whole does not produce the oil. The oil is ours, extracted from the bowels of our land and transported thousands of miles away to develop and nurture the empires of a corrupt oligarchy, thinking that the distance makes them safe. Now we have forced them to realise that their safety lies in ensuring social security and justice for the Niger Delta.

Look-Out rushes into the room.

Look-Out. General, there is a police patrol van in the street. We have to leave now! *(Marshall and Zino fan out immediately, covering Nari.)*

Nari. *(To Adesuwa, angrily)* What is this about?

Adesuwa. *(Recoiling)* It's a routine patrol. We pay the police to patrol our street once a week.

Nari. *(In disgust)* You pay the police to do their work? Nigeria, we hail thee!

Marshall. *(Trying to hustle Nari out)* We know of the patrol, but routine or not, let's leave, sir.

Zino. *(Pleading)* With due respect, this is becoming dangerous. Grasshoppers do not procrastinate by bidding each other farewell when the bush is on fire.

Nari. *(To Adesuwa, with a bow)* It was nice spending time with you, and I hope to read your interview soon … and by the way, I did not move into your building; your new neighbour was picked up by my boys yesterday. He is safe and sound and will be released to his family soon. No ransom was demanded. No ransom will be paid. Sorry for the inconvenience. *(To Iyobosa)* A word of caution: he is a reformed 419 kingpin; you may have to be a bit careful with this one.

Zino. Please understand that the goat is agitated over its owner's ailing health not out of love or compassion but out of self-preservation. If the owner recovers from the illness, there will be a feast; if he dies, there will be a funeral. Good-bye.

Nari. *(To Adesuwa).* You really need to change the lock on your door. *(They exit.)*

Iyobosa. *(Dreamily)* He is kind of cute.

Lights go to black while a follow spotlight picks out the bar. Narrator, Ben, and Orji are seated, with Ben and Orji leaning towards Narrator, apparently listening attentively.

Ben. *(Rising from his seat, stretching) Oh boy!* Crude oil's biggest damage to Nigeria is the encouragement of national indolence. Zero productivity.

Orji. *Gbam! (Rising angrily)* Our definition of productivity is the monthly trip to Abuja by commissioners of finance to collect their state's share of the oil revenue.

Narrator. *(Rising to join Ben and Orji. The three move around randomly, with movement, light effects, and insinuated sound effects depicting confusion.)* That is why when over three hundred thousand factory workers lost their jobs in 2009, nobody batted an eyelid.

Ben. What of the over ten thousand people that lost their jobs in the banking industry within the same period?

Orji. *Ewkuzina! (Lurching, genuflecting drunkenly)* This is a society where there is no social welfare. The laid-off workers, if they were lucky, probably got three months' salary in lieu of notice.

Narrator. *(Joining Orji on his feet)* Why wouldn't people think that crime is more rewarding than hard work?

Orji. *Bifor nko! (Still wavering on his feet)* It is only a foolish slave who, while pounding yam for his master, is licking his lips in anticipation of a feast.

Ben. That's why people grab, steal all they can, once they have the opportunity—because the terror of what their past has done to them presents them with a distorted view of the future.

Narrator. In a world of 6.9 billion people, Nigeria has a population of 150 million. In a world that has 212 million unemployed, Nigeria officially accounts for 40 million unemployed.

Ben. *You see!* It means that 20 percent of the world's unemployed are in Nigeria, while we account for just 2 percent of the world's population.

Narrator. As you would say, Ben, correct! To put it in better perspective, 40 million is about half the population of Germany, more than twice the population of the Netherlands, and more than the population of neighbouring Ghana.

Orji. *(Depressed) Nna men!* Where did we miss it?

Ben. *(Gloomily)* The country held so much promise before independence.

Narrator. Today we have become a pariah state, the product of a wasted generation ... a country that nobody wants to identify with, not even its citizens.

Ben. Every day our people throng all the foreign embassies in Nigeria seeking exit visas.

Orji. Don't even go there. Now, even when you want to travel abroad for legitimate reasons, you are viewed with suspicion.

Ben. Oh boy! It's the tragedy of maladministration that forces a people to a voluntary neocolonialism.

Narrator. This time around, we—me and you—have built and designed the slave ships, shackled ourselves in leg irons, and willingly sold our souls to the rest of the world.

Orji. *Nna* but why can't our government address poverty?

Ben. Why do they want us to believe that governance is rocket science, that leadership is the birthright of a select few?

Narrator. How come we have been recycling the same leaders since independence fifty years ago?

Orji. Leaders whose ideas and methods have become so ancient and stale that they better belong to the moribund National Museum.

(The random motions stop suddenly. Ben and Orji are frozen, and only Narrator is highlighted by a spotlight).

Narrator. *(Calmly, talking to the audience)* What we face is a crisis that can be seen in the spread of violence, corruption at all levels, and the general anger in the land. That anger is something we know well, the feeling that something was promised us but never received. The anger of unfulfillment ...

Black. Action moves back to centre stage. A blue spotlight picks out Iyobosa and Prophet on the couch. The table is set with food, wine, and several lit candles.)

Iyobosa. *(Reproachfully) Why ya bodi dey shake like leaf?*

Prophet. *(Visibly shaking) Ohh,* Iyobosa! The first time I set my eyes on you, I knew you were sent from heaven.

Iyobosa. *(Stroking his beard, his chest) Abeg!*

Prophet. True. *(Kneeling in front of her in a fever of ecstasy)* With my anointing, discerning such things comes naturally ... usually a slight tingling in my divining rod.

Iyobosa. *(Pulling him to his feet)* You have a divining rod? That sounds very ... macho. *(Teasingly) When I go see this rod?* Before or after my visa is ready?

Prophet. *(Hyperventilating)* Before and after, my Iyobosa, before and after.

Iyobosa. Hmm! That sounds nice *(casually detaching herself from his embrace), but I for like see the travel documents first,* then the divining rod.

Prophet. *(Following her, arms outstretched, like a lamb on a tether)* Come on, you mean you don't trust me?

Iyobosa. *(Sidestepping him)* Of course I do, Your Eminence.

Prophet. *(In hot pursuit)* Don't play hard to get. I know you want it as much as I do.

Iyobosa. *(Halts; angrily) Wetin you mean?*

Prophet. *(Grinning, like a little schoolboy)* You know what I mean. From the very first time I set my eyes on you, you have been wriggling your bottom at me, thrusting out your chest, throwing yourself at me. Setting my soul on fire.

Iyobosa. In due course, Your Eminence. *Sofri sofri.*

Prophet. *(Regaining his senses, surveying his environment)* But, are you sure we are okay here? Wouldn't we look stupid if your cousin walks in on us like this? Don't you think we should go to a hotel? I know this nice …

Iyobosa. Don't bother, Your Eminence. Adesuwa has gone for a press conference and won't be back before midnight.

Prophet. That's a bit comforting …

Iyobosa. *(Pulling him close)* So, my dear, please don't spoil this romantic mood.

Prophet. *(Pulls away)* To tell you the truth, I feel anything but romantic; here we are in Adesuwa's house, with the lights out …

Iyobosa. *(Helpfully)* We have candles.

Prophet. *(Still worried)* That's why I'm worried: drawn curtains and lit candles at four o'clock in the evening?

Iyobosa. Anyone but you should be complaining. You have lit candles in your church during the day as well.

Prophet. That is different.

Iyobosa. *(Slight pause; pensive)* Can't you feel it?

Prophet. *(Unsure)* Feel what?

Iyobosa. *(Teasingly)* Come on, the romance in the air?

Prophet. *(Slight pause)* To be honest, all I can feel is the tingling of my divining rod and the smell of melting wax. *(She pulls him close, and he moans in her embrace.)* Iyobosa!

The door opens, and Iyobosa and Prophet spring apart. Adesuwa enters.

Prophet. *(Embarrassed; straightening his frock)* I should leave now.

Adesuwa. (*Pauses as she notices Prophet*) Don't I know you?

Iyobosa. Yes, you do, this is Prophet.

Prophet. (*Crosses himself*) How are you, my daughter? You are truly blessed. Iyobosa has told me so much about your social crusades.

Adesuwa. (*Sarcastically, while opening the curtains*) And I assume that this little frolic is your contribution towards my social crusades?

There is a knock on the door.

Prophet. (*Seeing an opportunity to escape*) I will get it. (*Dashes out the door. Narrator/Greg enters, bedecked in his leather jacket, sporting a Bluetooth earpiece, earrings, gold rings, and gold chain with a huge pendant.*)

Narrator/Greg. I hope I'm not disturbing anything. Greg Ovia, your new neighbour.

Adesuwa. (*Wearily*) Let's hope that you are for real this time.

Greg. (*Apologetically*) I heard about your run-in with General Tinker-Tailor and his boys.

Iyobosa. (*Snuffing out the candles*) I hope they didn't hurt you.

Greg. On the contrary, they treated me fine. I understand it was you they were after. The boys in the creeks hold you in very high esteem and are all adherents of your publication. It is a pleasure to finally meet you in person. Can I borrow a mop and a bucket?

Iyobosa. Sure. (*She exits in search of a mop and bucket.*).

Adesuwa. (*Waving him to a seat, takes a seat herself*) So, how do you like the neighbourhood?

Greg. Aside from the scare from General Tinker-Tailor, nice, so far.

Adesuwa. (*Belligerently*) This is a very nice neighbourhood, a young population, all striving to make ends meet legitimately. To the best of my knowledge, no fraudster lives here, at least not yet.

Greg. (*Cautiously; rising*) What did you hear?

Adesuwa. (*Also rising*) Enough to get me worried.

Greg. That was in my past. If you notice, this is not exactly a neighbourhood for the rich and famous.

Iyobosa. *(Enters and hands Greg a mop and bucket)* You should have your wife do this.

Greg. How do you know I'm married? Oh! My wedding ring, of course. I wear it in memory of my wife.

Iyobosa. *(Coquettishly)* I'm so sorry.

Greg. It's all right. *(To Adesuwa)* I have read your publication. You really are a firebrand. May I sit *(slight pause)* again?

Adesuwa. Yes, please. *(Slight pause)* So what? You want to tell me why a fraudster …

Greg. I am a legitimate businessman now.

Adesuwa. *(Obstinately)* Okay, an ex-fraudster.

Iyobosa. *(Trying to make peace)* We are all tired and irritable. Can't this wait for another day?

Greg. *(Rising)* Is this another of your feature stories? I guess we might as well get it over with. Adesuwa, do you know what it means to have a commonwealth education?

Adesuwa. *(Barely interested)* Go on; I'm listening.

Greg. When, for the clan to survive, all of the clan's resources are channelled to one person, a torchbearer, who then has the responsibility of dragging the clan out of the doldrums. *(Pauses)* I was born the first male child in a family of nine children. My late father was an employee of the Ministry of Agriculture, specifically, a palm products officer. I am sure you have never heard of such an office before.

Adesuwa. *(Warming up to the story)* No, I haven't.

Greg. They went into the hinterlands, bought up palm products, and exported them on behalf of the government.

Adesuwa. That must have been before the oil boom.

Greg. With the euphoria of the oil boom, the country abandoned agriculture, and the jobs of the palm products officers became obsolete. My father's skills became obsolete.

Adesuwa. What has all this got to do with a commonwealth education?

Greg. By the time he retired from the service, his paltry retirement benefits and gratuity were only sufficient to train one out of his nine children through the university.

Iyobosa. That was you?

Greg. That was me. It became my lot to study hard, graduate from the university, and fend for my aged parents and my young siblings.

Adesuwa. *(Contemptuously)* The story of many Nigerian families. That is still no license to turn to crime.

Greg. You must be joking! What was I to turn to? Four years after I graduated from the university, there was no job in sight. My siblings were becoming increasingly antagonistic; many thought that they could have done better if Father's gratuity was spent on their university education. I needed money, and I needed money fast.

Iyobosa. Adesuwa will tell you that money is not everything.

Greg. Agreed that money is not everything, but it comes very close to being everything. Ask people who don't have it.

Adesuwa. It is people like you that destroy the moral fabric of this country.

Greg. *(Vehemently)* Really? I don't owe the country anything. Nigeria owes me big time! I wasted four years looking for a job after I left the university. I lost two years at the university due to the incessant strike actions by our lecturers. I wasted one year in the mandatory one-year National Youth Service Programme. I lost a total of seven years of my life. The cruellest joke of all was that all the decent companies in the country will not hire a fresh graduate who is above twenty-four years old. There I was at twenty-five years, staring at a very bleak future.

Iyobosa. *Haba! But 419 no good na!*

Greg. *(Heading towards the exit)* Let's just say that at that point, I decided not to leave my destiny in another man's hands.

Adesuwa. *(Blocking his retreat)* Even though your actions caused others anguish?

Greg. *(Confrontationally)* It was self-help. My only route out of poverty, as I could see no help coming from our corrupt leaders.

Adesuwa. You know, when people accuse our leaders of corruption, I usually tell them that corruption is only a symptomatic manifestation of the problem. Our problem is a lack of respect for other individuals' right to life. When you drive someone to death by swindling his hard-earned savings; the morally corrupt trader, who sells adulterated drugs to the public, knowing full well that any patient who ingests the drugs has purchased a ticket to the afterlife; the contractor who is paid to construct a road and builds it with substandard material, knowing full well that failed sections of the road will ultimately lead to road accidents and death; the politician who corners funds meant to develop his community, better his people, knowing that that water borehole would have supplied the people with much-needed potable water or that cottage hospital would have provided our mothers, our fathers, our brothers and sisters with much-needed health care without which people would die. No, my dear, our problem is not corruption; it is a pathological lack of respect for our brothers' right to life, the right to a decent life.

Greg. You cannot equate what we did to the unbridled corruption of our leaders! At least the money we got was reinvested in our economy.

Adesuwa. *(Indignantly)* The opprobrium from your international Robin Hood activities comes back to us in Nigeria.

Greg. Whose Nigeria? Their Nigeria or our Nigeria? Both the leaders and we the led don't even believe in the country.

Iyobosa. *Adesuwa believes in this country sha. With her over sabi, I no sabi why she never go contest election.*

Greg. Because she can't afford to. Politics in Nigeria is expensive. It is only in Nigeria that you have people whose only source of livelihood is politics. Hear them, *(Mimicking a journalist with a microphone)* So, what do you do for a living, sir? *(Posing as the politician)* I am a grassroots politician.

Adesuwa. What kind of job is that?

Greg. The premise of a country is its citizens. People who are willing to live and die in the defence of the country. We do not have such people, in fact, we do not have citizens of Nigeria. We have Ijaw citizens, Hausa citizens, Fulanis, Yorubas, Igbos, Kanuris … we do not have Nigerian citizens, so there is no sense of collective ownership. When Americans, Britons, citizens of other countries are protesting against their government, they burn their nation's flag. Have you ever seen a Nigerian burn our national flag in protest? Of course not! The flag holds no meaning to us, does not serve as a binding force. No, Ma, it doesn't. That is the tragedy of Nigeria.

Iyobosa. General Tinker-Tailor is willing to die for something he believes in.

Adesuwa. Nigerians may readily kill for a cause but are not known to die for any cause.

Iyobosa. We can spend the rest of the day drinking *panadol* for Nigeria, and nothing we say or do here will have any impact. Greg, why don't you come over for dinner? I am sure Adesuwa wouldn't mind, and then we can listen to your story over a good meal.

Adesuwa. I believe that what Greg needs is a good night's rest.

Iyobosa. *Haba!* On an empty stomach? I'm sure he hasn't eaten anything this evening. *(Coquettishly)* Will you come over, please?

Greg. *(Relieved for the change in subject)* Sounds like a great idea. Say, why don't I take you ladies out for dinner?

Iyobosa. *(Excitedly)* Excellent! That sounds great.

Adesuwa. *(Wearily)* Iyobosa, you and Greg should go along. I've had a pretty tiring day.

Greg. *(Pleading)* Come on, you don't have any early morning appointment tomorrow. Besides, I am not planning to stay out late.

Adesuwa. But …

Greg. No buts. I'll give you some time to freshen up…. Will be back in a couple of minutes. *(Greg exits.)*

Iyobosa. What are we waiting for? You heard him; let's get dressed.

Adesuwa. *(Cautiously)* I don't like the way you sound.

Iyobosa. What have I done again?

Adesuwa. Iyobosa, if you are getting dressed, please get dressed.

Iyobosa. Of course, I'll get dressed.

Adesuwa. No, you will not. Anytime you talk about getting dressed, you end up more undressed than dressed.

Iyobosa. *(Combatively)* If you don't want me to come along, why don't you just say so?

Adesuwa. Why wouldn't I want you to come along? I didn't want to go in the first instance. Still don't want to go.

Greg. *(From outside)* Ladies, are you ready?

Iyobosa. *(Goes to the door)* Give us twenty minutes.

Greg. All right, twenty minutes. I'm counting.

Light fades to black as Adesuwa and Iyobosa enter the bedroom. A follow-spotlight picks out Narrator, Orji, and Ben at the bar.

Orji. *Nna men!* *(Shaking his head in amazement)* No wonder you have all the details. I didn't see that one coming.

Ben. *(Reproachfully)* Hope you have left the 419 business?

Narrator. Once I turned legit, I never looked back. There were tough times, but I have survived.

Ben. *Oh boy,* you are a correct man. Barman! Another bottle of Star for our new friend, Mr. Greg.

Narrator. Thank you.

Ben. Listening to your story reiterates my fear that we have failed as a people.

Orji. *Gbam! Gbachi fa nkiti!* After, they will blame the global financial meltdown. Now every failure in the system is caused by the global financial meltdown, whereas we all know that Nigeria was already in the throes of Churg-Strauss syndrome, multiple organ failure, long before the global crisis.

Narrator. Our country is dying a slow and painful arsenic death. The mass of impoverished individuals threaten the very existence of the successful few. The price for success this few have to pay is that they and their families are kidnapped for ransom, randomly killed as a sign of protest, anger. So the country suffers, and people are no longer safe in the land; people are now afraid to be successful lest they be singled out as a symbol of the oppressing class and butchered.

The Manchester United fan walks past again, hooting, 'Up Man U'.

Orji. *Ewu town council!* See them. Over the weekends several Nigerian big men jet out to the United Kingdom just to watch an English Premiership football match.

Ben. Correct!

Orji. Yet none, not even one of them, can muster the courage to see a football match live in any of the mostly derelict stadia that we have in this country. *Igasikwa!*

Ben. *Oh boy why you dey vex?* That is no different from the rest of our elite, who rush abroad to treat the simplest ailments while they are not bothered that the general hospitals back home have become mortuaries.

Narrator. *(Rising to his feet)* But you know what? The biggest failure is in the education sector. If you walk onto the shop floor of Nigeria's commercial banks, major telecommunications companies, and oil companies, you will see a mass of Nigeria's best and brightest. First-class and second-class upper graduates of our universities.

Orji. *Gbam!* You are absolutely right.

Narrator. Typically, in a sane society, some of these students will be retained as lecturers by their university.

Ben. *Haba my guy!* Working in our moribund education sector cannot put food on their table; the pay is simply miserable.

Narrator. So, here you have potential research fellows, scientists, engineers, doctors, yes doctors, grossly suboptimised. But the real tragedy is that those who end up applying for the university jobs are the ones who simply couldn't make the cut in the lucrative oil and gas, telecommunications, and banking sectors. That is the real tragedy.

Orji. *Nna men! (Banging his fist on the table and rising angrily)* What is wrong with our people? I am angry!

Ben. What for?

Orji. For the unfulfilled dreams that our parents shared with us post-independence.

Narrator. I am angry for my country, Nigeria has become a 150-million-man nursery of talents for other nations, since we cannot cater for our own.

Ben. *Oh boy! Me sef I dey vex!*

Spotlight fades on the bar, and action moves back to centre stage. A blue spotlight picks out Iyobosa and Adesuwa as they enter the house.

Iyobosa. *(Gushing)* That joint was hot. Did you notice how all the guys were staring at us?

Adesuwa. *(Angrily)* They were not staring at us. They were staring at you. And you didn't have to take off your jacket. I should have known that it was too good to be true when you appeared in that jacket. The heat was simply an excuse to reveal this skimpy thing you had underneath.

Iyobosa. Why do you always put me under an electron microscope?

Adesuwa. *(Sniffing the air)* You didn't smoke here, did you?

Iyobosa. You know I don't smoke.

Adesuwa. Then who did?

Zino. *(Switching on the light)* An irony, but I have always been scared of the dark.

Iyobosa. Commander Zino!

Adesuwa. I thought I sighted you at the press conference.

Zino. Yes, you did. I was monitoring proceedings at your press conference. But you know what they say, 'there is no justice for a slave in a court presided over by the slave master'. The chicken are always found guilty at the tribunal of foxes.

Iyobosa. It appears that you thrive on dangerous situations. You could have been captured.

Zino. At the time, I believed it was pretty safe, as aside from you two, no one could match a face to the name Commander Zino.

Adesuwa. So, what do you want from me now? I have kept my side of the bargain. I ran the story you wanted, called a press conference on your behalf—what else do you want?

Zino. Nothing. This time I am the one who will do you a favour.

Iyobosa. What do you mean?

Zino. *(Somberly)* A soldier must be prepared for either of two things: victory or defeat, life or death. *(Slight pause)* General Tinker-Tailor is dead.

Adesuwa. What!

Iyobosa. *Osanobua!*

Zino. Yes. They finally got him. They claim he was cut down in a cross fire during his attempt to storm the governor's lodge—a claim I find preposterous. General did not need to storm the governor's lodge. He was a regular visitor there. Information reaching me is that Commander Marshall was a government mole. He talked so much about the havoc reactionaries were wreaking on the struggle, yet he was the real reactionary, a bloody traitor!

Iyobosa. Commander Marshal killed the general?

Zino. It appears so. The details are still sketchy, but what is clear is that the general is dead.

Silence.

Adesuwa. So, what now?

Zino. When a great tree falls, little and big birds fly away. I am worried for you. The government will clamp down on real or perceived loyalists of the general, you included. You have to run.

Iyobosa. They can't do anything to her. This is a democracy, not an authoritarian regime.

Zino. Are you kidding? The shrieking of a fowl does not stop a sacrifice. The drummer who plays on even when the burial ceremony is over is either serenading the widow of the deceased or wants to join the deceased. I am on my way out of the country, and I advise you to do the same. Don't bother with your publication; for all intents and purposes, it is dead, unless you can revive it from outside the country.

Adesuwa. What do you mean?

Zino. I have it on good authority that the government has asked all your corporate sponsors to pull out their business with you; otherwise, they stand being charged with trumped-up crimes. You need to move, and you need to move fast. As for me, I am out of here. Would have been long gone, but thought we owed you one; after all, you didn't ask to be dragged into this fight. Please take my advice. An animal that insists on dancing upon sighting a hunter has made a pact with death. Goodnight. (Exits.)

Adesuwa. *(Petrified)* This must be a cruel joke. *(Her cell phone rings)* Hello. Yes, I have just been informed. *(Pause as the party on the other side appears to be talking)* So, what do you want me to do? Okay. I understand. Thank you, sir.

Iyobosa. *(Anxiously)* So?

Adesuwa. I have just been told by one of my sources to lay low, vamoose, disappear!

Iyobosa. *Which kind thing be this?* Disappear?

Adesuwa. Disappear, vanish, go underground. They think that I have General Tinker-Tailor's confidence. It appears that the authorities think he shared with me the real relationship that exists between them. Now that he is dead, some people want me out of the way as well.

Iyobosa. *Which kind wahala be dis?* This means we need to move fast.

Adesuwa. I am sure that we are already under observation. *(Suddenly remembering)* Greg. We need Greg to smuggle me out of the house in his car. From there, I will find my way to Ghana, Togo, or Benin Republic, and hibernate till this blows over.

Iyobosa. *Madam Boy's-Quarters dey go Benin Republic well-well.* Let's talk to her.

Adesuwa. You are right. I can use this period of hibernation to do some investigative journalism as well, write a story on Madam Boy's-Quarters' racket.

Iyobosa. *Abeg I no fit shout! Na to hide we wan make you hide, no be to go make wahala for Madam Boy's-Quarters and Prophet.*

Adesuwa. *(Confidently)* Trust me. I will be fine, a natural survivor if ever there was one.

Iyobosa. *(Pleading)* Then at least let me come along with you.

Adesuwa. Travelling with me will only increase the risk of us being discovered.

Iyobosa. *How? Person wey fit see you alone go fit see both of us.*

Adesuwa. *(After a brief pause)* I honestly don't understand your logic.

Iyobosa. *Wetin you mean?*

Adesuwa. Never mind. I need to buy me a crucial twenty-four hours. That is all I need, twenty-four hours.

Light fades to a blue spotlight on the bar. Ben and Orji are on their feet, watching Narrator with rapt attention.

Narrator. That was the catalyst that emboldened Adesuwa to embark on this adventure. So off she went in search of Prophet and Madam Boy's-Quarters. As if to ensure that she did not have time to change her mind, that same night, she and fourteen other young men and girls were hurried into a hired commercial bus at Mile 2 car park in Lagos and driven straight to the Seme border. Border formalities were expectedly easy, with Madam Boy's-Quarters greasing the palms of the immigrations officials on both the Nigerian side of the border and on the Benin Republic side, as if a case of, 'what is good for the goose is also good for the gander'.

From the border, all of them were taken to the Jonquet area of Cotonou, down a winding alley, into a long, dimly lit, damp, smelly corridor in what looked like an abandoned, windowless warehouse.

A bare room, with the sole furniture being a low, long altar, around which are lit candles of different colours. The altar is surrounded by a circle of young men and women (dressed as if embarking on a long journey), swinging to an undulating chant led by an incense-burner-swinging Prophet. Prophet is barefoot, has no shirt on, and is sporting what appears to be a red frock over a pair of white trousers. Madam Boy's-Quarters is seen directing proceedings.

Prophet. Madam Boy's-Quarters, please lead us in a prayer for journey mercies.

Madam Boy's-Quarters. *(Thundering)* Praise the Lord!

Congregation. Hallelujah.

Madam Boy's-Quarters. *(Waving at the congregation with one hand, very carefully, deliberately adjusting her head tie with the other, and swinging her backside as she approaches the altar)* Praaaaaaaaise the Lord!

Congregation. Hallelujah!

Madam Boy's-Quarters. *(Moving about with energy) Osanobua! Baba!* The almighty and everlasting *Baba. We taink you ohh!* King of kings and Lord of lords. *We dey taink you ohh!* God of all creation, *na our tine be this!*

Congregation. *Yes ohh!* Amen!

Madam Boy's-Quarters. *Yes ohh! Na our tine be this! (Moves around, intermittently waving her hands and touching members of the congregation)* We honour and bless your name for you too kind, *Baba!* You too faithful, *Baba!* We thank you for the gift of life in the name of Jah.

Congregation. Amen!

Madam Boy's-Quarters. When your son David cried out to you *(slight pause) Baba! Na ya face e dey find Baba! (Another slight pause) Na so we sef de find ya face today Baba. Monkey smart, monkey smart, na because say tree near tree.* We need your help, *Baba.* We dream of you, *Baba.* We remember that all things belong to you, *Baba.* In the name of Jah, we pray!

Congregation. Amen!

Madam Boy's-Quarters. *Osanobua don hear una prayers, na why e send me* Yes ohh! Let us pray for your sponsors. *These beta travel agents, wey be say, for small, small money, chicken change, go carry una enter Europe.* Just as Joshua sent his agents into the Promised Land, *na so dem go send una enter beta place. Abeg make una clap for these wonderful people!*

The congregation claps wholeheartedly.

Madam Boy's-Quarters. Amen!

Congregation. Amen!

Prophet. *(Looking straight up)* Listen to their pleas, oh Lord! For they come before you in light of your promises: You will make a way when there seems to be no way. Give us the ability to create wealth, make money, more than we can ever imagine. Please have mercy on us, oh Lord! *(Crosses himself)* Madam Boy's-Quarters. *Abeg* prayer for journey mercies.

Madam Boy's-Quarters. *(Crosses herself).* In the name of Jah.

Congregation. Amen!

Madam Boy's-Quarters. *(Moving about with energy and flailing her arms) Ose Baba! God I taink you ohh!* I commit this journey into your hands, oh Lord! The lives of your children here with me, I also commit into your able care. I decree that your angels will go before them in the name of Jah!

Congregation. Amen!

Madam Boy's-Quarters. Ah! *Baba! (Pause)* Any weapon of darkness fashioned by our enemies against us will backfire in the mighty name of Jah!

Congregation. Amen!

Madam Boy's-Quarters. *(Slight pause)* I take authority over the road and decree journey mercies in Jesus' name.

Congregation. Amen!

Madam Boy's-Quarters. *(Enthralled)* We cover our route with the blood of Jesus. From Nigeria to Benin Republic, Togo, Burkina Faso, Mali, Niger, Libya, and finally, Spain and Italy.

Congregation. *(Break out in frenzied choruses of 'Amen!')*

Madam Boy's-Quarters. Praise the Lord!

Congregation. Hallelujah!

Madam Boy's-Quarters. *(Moving about in a frenzy) Ya pillar of fire go dey guide us for night! Na ya pillar of smoke go protect us for day!* We will conquer Seme, drive through Krake, finish Cotonou, chop for Quidah, run things for Dohi, drink tombo for Agatogbo, rest for Gadome, come and see Come, poh-poh for Grand Popo, and sleep for Hilla Condji.

Congregation. Amen!

Madam Boy's-Quarters. From Bamako to Fana to Segou to Bla to Mopti to Sevare to Douanza to Gossi, Gao, Agadez. *Yes oh! Na ya pillar of fire by night! Then ya pillar of smoke go come guide us by day!* Every stop, every city we pass through will be covered by the blood of Jah! Let Morocco and Spain be our anointing in Jah's blessed name, we pray!

Congregation. *(A thunderous 'Amen!')*

Madam Boy's-Quarters. *(Indignantly, but laughingly)* And for those that murmur: What will we do when we get there? *How we go take survive?* What skills do we have? *Abi na Ashewo work de wan make we do?* Do they want us to be prostitutes? Are they sending us to steal? *Na wetin sef? Which wan be their own? Make dem look inside holy book! Na who save Israelite spies for Jericho? Na Rahab the harlot*! Who was the ancestor of King David? It was Ruth, *the despised Moabitess.* Who saved Nigeria from the dark-goggled general with a poisoned apple, straight from the Garden of Eden? *Na* woman, especially imported from India. That's right! *No mind them joo!* Your sacrifices will free your families from poverty. In Jah's mighty name, we pray!

Congregation. *(Choruses of 'Amen!' and 'Praise the Lord!')* *(Prophet is seen laying out an array of items on the table. These include a gourd, a bottle of local gin, alligator pepper, kola nuts, and white chalk.)*

Prophet. *(Smiles broadly at no one in particular)* As an additional spiritual insurance to our supplications to Jah, we call on the spirits of our ancestors to help forestall possible arrest and repatriation from Europe.

Madam Boy's-Quarters. Ise!

Prophet. *(Crosses himself)* Brrrhh! Aaargh! Zanzibar! *(Moving about with energy)* We also remember the kindheartedness of our sponsors who have undertaken to send you to the Promised Land. We call on our goddess Ayelala! Ayelala! The slave woman who was wrongfully killed and now takes her vengeance from the great beyond. She who cannot be perjured, as her perjurers perish within a week. *(The congregation begins to visibly cringe.)* *(Crosses himself)* Brrrrhhh! Aaargh! Zanzibar! Ayelala! I bring these children before you, for those who partake in eating sacrifices made to the gods surely owe the gods. Bind them by their words and bring the fear of your wrath to their conscience. You that cannot be bribed! No *mago-mago*, no awaiting trial! Death! Madness and painful death to your transgressors!

Madam Boy's-Quarters. *(Moving about with energy and flailing her arms)* Ise!

Prophet. You *(pointing to a lady in the congregation)*, come forward, come here, my daughter. What is your name?

Madam Boy's-Quarters. *Na Ivie,* Your Eminence.

Prophet. Ivie. Brrrrrhhh! Aaargh! Zanzibar! What a beautiful name, my daughter. Do you know what your name means?

Ivie. It means Jewel, Your Eminence.

Madam Boy's-Quarters. *(Avidly)* Something of great value.

Prophet. *(Scrutinizes her carefully)* Yes, my dear. You may not have brought great value along at your birth, but today I decree that you have found wealth; you will bring wealth to your family, my daughter.

Congregation Chorus. *Ise!*

Prophet. So tell me, do you really desire to go to Europe? Do you truly want to shed the shackles of poverty and destitution?

Ivie. *(Enthusiastically)* Yes! Yes, Your Eminence.

Prophet. Kneel. *(Ivie hurriedly goes down on her knees)* Touch this gourd to your forehead three times *(hands her a gourd from the table)*. That's right; now touch it to your chest three times. *(Enthralled)* Now repeat after me: I am the beneficiary of my sponsor's kindness.

Ivie. *(Gushing)* I am the beneficiary of my sponsor's kindness.

Prophet. With my own mouth and soul …

Ivie. With my own mouth and soul …

Prophet. I hereby invite the great Ayelala …

Ivie. I hereby invite the great Ayelala …

Prophet. To visit me with the most potent misfortune and death …

Ivie. To visit me with the most potent misfortune and death …

Prophet. Should I under any circumstance reveal my kindhearted sponsor's plans to the police, immigration, or any other government authority …

Ivie. Should I under any circumstance reveal my kindhearted sponsor's plans to the police, immigration, or any other government authority …

Prophet. Or should I fail to remit to the last dollar owed to my kindhearted sponsor, as soon as I begin to earn money.

Ivie. Or should I fail to remit to the last dollar owed to my kindhearted sponsor, as soon as I begin to earn money.

Prophet. To seal this pact, we need ashes of your fingernail cuttings, ashes of your pubic hair, and eyelashes.

Madam Boy's-Quarters. *(Hands over an envelope to Prophet)* Here you are, Your Eminence.

Prophet. (*Scrutinizes the contents of the envelope carefully and bursts suddenly into a peal of raucous laughter*) A child who inherits his father's *Babariga* does not appreciate the value of the attire. (*Pacing*) A lizard may resemble a crocodile, but their bite size clearly differentiates them. As the crocodile is shy to bite, when it does bite, it is extremely shy to let go. (*Pours the content of the envelope into the gourd. Takes Ivie's right hand and, with a razor blade, makes three quick incisions*) By this blood that you spill in this gourd (*drips the blood into the gourd*), the heat of gin and alligator pepper (*sloshes some gin into the gourd, followed by alligator pepper*), your pubic hair (*points the gourd at her pubic region*), that guardian to your canal of procreation, fingernails (*dips her finger in the gourd*), the forerunner of everything you touch, and your eyelashes (*points the gourd in this direction*), that which seals and opens the portals through which you view the world. Drink from this gourd, drink! Drink!

Madam Boy's-Quarters. (*Nodding affirmatively with a smile*) Drink!

Congregation Chorus. *Drink! Drink! Drink!* (*Ivie squeamishly drinks the concoction and is ushered to her seat by Madam Boy's-Quarters. Her gait suggests some form of intoxication.*)

Prophet. Well done, Ivie. I can see that the spirit is moving you already. Your father will be very proud of you. He specifically requested that I make sure you do not disappoint him, that you make him proud. You will see for yourself. Within twelve months from today, you will be able to not only buy him the car that he desires so much but also build a modest, modern bungalow in Benin.

Congregation Chorus. *Ise!*

Prophet. And that is only if you want to be modest, for by then you will be able to afford a sprawling mansion, your very own, white house. Complete with a beautiful garden and a playground for your children.

Congregation Chorus. *Ise!*

Prophet. No man can climb to a rooftop without a ladder. This is your ladder, the moment you have been waiting for. Grab the opportunity with both hands! Who else wants to be like Ivie? Who else is willing to embark on this great journey of self-discovery with us? Who? You? (*Pointing at the other men and women*) You? What of you?

Adesuwa. (*Steps forward*) I do.

Madam Boy's-Quarters. (*Clearing her throat*) Your Eminence, *this wan na bad market. She no gree give us her somethings.*

Prophet. *Her somethings?*

Madam Boy's-Quarters. *Yes.*

Prophet. (*Crosses himself*) Brrrrrrh! Aaargh! Zanzibar! *Who be dat?*

Adesuwa. (*Calmly, indignantly*) With all due respect, Your Eminence, my religion does not permit me to engage in blood rituals with my body parts.

Madam Boy's-Quarters. (*With rising agitation*) Porca Vacca! (*Pronounced POR-kah VAH-kah*) Dammit! Who told you that we engage in *bloody* rituals? This is a covenant.

Prophet. (*Calmly*) Okay, Madam Boy's-Quarters. (*Turning to Adesuwa*) What faith do you profess? Christianity, I suppose. Do you think I am not a Christian? I am a prophet of the Living God, a Shepherd of the good Lord's flock.

Adesuwa. (*Obstinately*) Running a church does not make you a Christian, just as standing in a kitchen does not make you a cook.

Madam Boy's-Quarters. (*In an uncontrolled outburst*) Merda! (*Pronounced MEHR-dah*) Shit! I said it! *You be bad market. Bring your something you no bring! Drink from the gourd you no drink! Na only you?*

Adesuwa. (*Staring at the gourd suspiciously*) That gourd contains human blood and God knows what else. No, thank you.

Prophet. (*Thundering*) Drink it now! Drink!

Madam Boy's-Quarters. (*Exploding at her*) Oya! Drink it now! Drink! (*Pushes the gourd forcibly to her lips, but Adesuwa breaks away, backing away from her*)

Congregation Chorus. *Drink! Drink! Drink!*

Light fades to three spotlights focused on Adesuwa, Narrator, and Ben and Orji. There appears to be a confluence between the characters at the bar and the story. This scene represents the turmoil in Adesuwa's mind.

Adeswua. *(In a soliloquy, stricken by sudden doubt)* What am I about to do?

Narrator. *(Warning)* Drinking that potion is a life sentence. It is spiked with drugs and is their first step towards keeping you a mental captive. Drop that gourd and walk away.

Adesuwa. *(Confused)* With what I have seen so far, I doubt that they will let me walk away.

Ben. Correct! Of course, they will not let you walk away.

Narrator. Adesuwa, don't mind him. You really don't want to do this.

Orji. *(Angrily) Nna go and sit down!* Don't do this! Don't do that! What other choice does she have?

Narrator. You always have a choice!

Adesuwa. I am a journalist, not a hungry, vulnerable immigrant. Once I have my story, I will escape.

Ben. *(Smiling, unbelieving) Okay now!* Let's wait and see.

Narrator. You already have all you need for the story. Please walk away, for these people are vicious.

Adesuwa. I can handle this.

Orji. *Ah ah! Egwu o na atukwa gi!* Run, Adesuwa! Run now; you still can! Just run!

The chant of 'Drink! Drink! Drink!' gains crescendo. Light fades on Narrator, Ben, and Orji; while the spotlight on Adesuwa flickers, depicting the turmoil in her mind. Full lights come back on amidst the now very loud chanting of 'Drink! Drink!'

Adesuwa. *(Raising her hand)* Stop! Prophet, I know what you are and what you want; I will not drink from this cup.

Prophet. *(Thundering in an uncontrolled outburst)* Aaargh! Zanzibar! Kill her!

Lights go to black.

Light slowly comes up to a blue spotlight on the bar.

Orji. *Nna wetin come happen?*

Ben. Oh boy! Don't tell me that they killed her!

Narrator. Let's leave the rest of the story for another day.

Orji. *Nna they kill am, abi they no kill am?*

Narrator. What good is a story if it doesn't have its twists and turns? I have to leave now; my wife is here. (*Adesuwa enters.*)

Black

THE END

Hell's Invitation

Characters

Aliyu

Stella

Emeka

Bimbo

Lateef

Tarasco

Sammy Coker

Papa Ruka

Groundnut Seller

Charity, Ify, and Uju

Scene I

A sparsely furnished one-room apartment dotted with old, cheap furniture: chairs with springs and stuffing spilling out of the cushions, a broken clothes rack, a rickety spring bed with no mattress, an old/spoilt television set, and a centre table. Most of the housemates are seen in various sleeping positions. Lateef is (topless) sleeping on the bed, while Aliyu, Stella, and Emeka are all sprawled, sleeping, on any available space.

The housemates are all university graduates in their early twenties. Aliyu is tall, amiable, dark, and lanky, with a noticeable Hausa accent. He seems very self-assured. Stella is authoritative, knowledgeable, quite pretty; her sexuality is like a visible colour on her. Emeka is powerfully built, loquacious and talks authoritatively in a strong Igbo accent, and wears his education on his sleeve. Lateef is short, stolid, and laconic.

As lights come on, Bimbo is illuminated, standing dressed in a flowing white 'Aladura' church robe. He is short, lithe, crafty, and street-smart.

Bimbo. *(Intoning)* Emeka! Emeka! Rise! Rise!

Emeka. *(Jumps up in fright)* Yeah! Yeah! Help! Help! Ghost! *(Running away from Bimbo, waking Stella and Aliyu in the process)* Help! Ghost!

(They all scramble in a blind rush away from Bimbo. Only Lateef remains sleeping).

Stella. What? Ghost? Ooh, my God! Where?

Aliyu. There it is!

Stella. Police! Call the police!

Bimbo. Hey! Hey! You guys should relax.

Aliyu. It's Bimbo.

Emeka. *(In exasperation)* Bimbo! What the hell are you doing dressed like this?

Bimbo. *(Expansively, with infinite patience)* Not Bimbo, but Brother Bimbo, of the Mountain of Fire, Lightning, and Prosperity Apostolic Mission, aka Tabernacle of Thunder fellowship.

Aliyu. *(In exasperation)* There you go again….

Stella. Is that why you scared us like that?

There is a loud banging on the door.

Aliyu. Who is it?

Papa Ruka. *(Offstage) Wetin dey happen? Na thief?*

Aliyu opens the door, and Papa Ruka rushes in brandishing a machete.

Aliyu. *(Swearing) Ka chi walahi!* It's no thief. This overgrown baby played a practical joke on us.

Bimbo. Who is an overgrown baby?

Papa Ruka. Thank God, *I think say na thief!*

Bimbo. *(Proselytizing)* So shall the Lord God of hosts creep upon you sinners like a thief in the night.

Papa Ruka. *(Angrily) Eeeh! That one na God abi? But if you try am for my side I go show you say I be proper OPC.*

Papa Ruka exits, slamming the door.

Bimbo. *(At Papa Ruka's disappearing back)* For it is written, 'Thou shall not raise your hand against the Lord's anointed'.

Stella. Bimbo, are you serious with this church thing?

Bimbo. *(Laughing)* Serious? My sister, this is our ticket to heaven!

Emeka. *(In disbelief)* See who is talking about heaven!

Bimbo. Actually, I meant, our meal ticket to heaven.

Aliyu. Please don't tell me you want to start a church.

Bimbo. And why not? Everybody does it these days. Look! It's the fastest means of making fast money; and you know, you don't need capital, you don't need collateral. It is almost like getting a microfinance loan to set up a small business *(slight pause)* just better.

Stella. *(In exasperation)* Bimbo, there you go again.

Bimbo. *(Excitedly)* The money is tax-free, no VAT, no withholding tax. Cool down! I have already done the feasibility study. See, this is the cash-flow projection and business plan. As you can see, it is credit, credit, credit all the way. No debit!

Aliyu. *(In disbelief)* You are not serious. Look at you! You want to start a church? Just like that?

Bimbo. *(Shrugging)* Just like that.

Aliyu. You must be kidding me. Okay, what denomination is this church of yours?

Bimbo. The Prosperity Communion!

Emeka. *(In disbelief)* Prosperity Communion?

Bimbo. *Yes Keh!* Relax. What we need is a room like this, a Bible, convincing speakers, and a congregation. The first three we already have, and it is just a matter of time before the congregation begins to pour in.

Emeka. *(Turning on Bimbo in an uncontrolled outburst) Akpi gba gi!* Nonsense! This is not only 419; it is the impersonation of a man of God. Such an act is punishable under section 484 of the criminal code of Nigeria, Laws of the Federation 1990.

Bimbo. *(Confidently)* Forget the law! This is money! Real money! *Ego!* Besides, who says the kingdom of heaven cannot be brought down to earth? With this kind of money, we'll all be living in heaven.

Aliyu. *(Swearing) Ka chi walahi!* You'll answer for this in heaven.

Bimbo. *(Confidently)* I'll wait till I get there.

Emeka. You can't get away with this. The law is neither an ass nor a donkey. Slow and steady, and it will surely catch up with you.

Bimbo. You think I didn't make provisions for that? Why do you think I have you, a law graduate of the University of Nigeria Nsukka, not only a *'Great Lion'* but the first lawyer, homegrown, mind you homegrown, not imported, of the Odenigbo clan. *Osi na Nwata buru Ogaranya!*

Emeka. *(Surprised, beaming)*You mean I am the company lawyer?

Bimbo. *(Condescendingly, spreading his hands expansively)* That sounds too secular, my friend, more like the 'MC', the mission counsel.

Emeka. *(Trying out his new title)* Barrister Emeka Obi, LLB Hons. MC, the Mission Counsel, Mountain of Fire, Lightning, and Prosperity Apostolic Mission, aka Tabernacle of Thunder Fellowship. Hmmm! Sounds impressive.

Stella. *(Turning her back on them)* I'll not be a party to this scam.

Bimbo. Suit yourself. At least you have a choice; you can starve to death.

Emeka. *(Pointing at the sleeping Lateef)* What of Lateef?

Bimbo. He can sleep on. At least with him here, we do not need a prophet; he is always in a trance.

Emeka. That's true.

Bimbo. *(Obviously in the spirit of the moment, moving about with energy, expressiveness)* Not enough to have just a preacher and a mission counsel. *(Moves towards Aliyu)* Not enough for the Lord. Now we need a treasurer, someone we trust, someone who can count our money, someone who will keep our money.

Emeka. *(Helpfully)* I can do two jobs.

Bimbo. *(Ignoring Emeka)* Any volunteers?

Aliyu. *(Brief hesitation)* I am not very good at figures, but if I am hired I wouldn't …

Bimbo. *(Puts his arm around Aliyu)* That's it, my guy! Just know the colour of the currency notes; the good Lord will teach you the rest.

Stella. *(Cynically)* If you want to pass for a man of God, don't you think you should know your Bible a bit better?

Bimbo. Stella your problem is that you are too conservative. These days all a preacher needs know about is prosperity.

Stella. *(Unsure)* Prosperity?

Bimbo. *(Moving about with energy)* My dear, people are depressed economically, socially, politically, and morally. All they need is someone who can convince them that their fortunes will change exponentially if they believe in God.

Stella. And that person is you?

Bimbo. Who better than me?

Aliyu. *(Impressed)* You have it all worked out.

Bimbo. Of course, I do.

Emeka. So, how do we get our customers? Oh, sorry, I meant our congregation?

Bimbo. Look at this! *(He unfurls a placard that proclaims the Mountain of Fire, Lightning, and Prosperity Apostolic Mission.)* We place this outside, while we praise and worship inside. Before long, we will have a full house.

Emeka. *(Excitedly)* So what are we waiting for?

They begin to sing, dance, prophesy, and cynically speak in tongues. The racket finally wakes Lateef up. Papa Ruka rushes in again, brandishing his machete as usual.

Papa Ruka. What is going on here?

Bimbo. *(Preaching, obviously in the spirit and twirling like a man possessed)* Papa Ruka! Brother Papa Ruka! The Lord has finally heard your prayers. He has clearly heard the supplication of his lost son, that is why! That is why he has used me as a point of contact to minister to you.

Papa Ruka. *(Angrily)* Bimbo! Is that not Bimbo? Will you stop this nonsense!

Bimbo. *(Enthralled, gesticulating widely, waving his hands in the air)* Papa Rukaaaaa! I know of your entire problems, Brother Papa Rukaaaaa!

At this point, anytime Papa Ruka opens his mouth, his words are drowned by the combined voices of Aliyu, Emeka, and Stella as they pray and speak in tongues.

Aliyu, Emeka, and Stella. *Robo! Scadarabababa! Robo!*

Bimbo. Of the money you owe Iya Zainab!

Aliyu, Emeka, and Stella. *Skarda! Robo! Robo!*

Bimbo. Of your unpaid house rent!

Emeka. *Puyaka! Puyaka!*

Bimbo. The Lord has heard your prayers and will answer you tenfold!

Aliyu, Emeka, and Stella. *Skanda! Robo! Skanda! Robo!*

There is a loud banging on the door.

Tarasco. *(Offstage) Person no fit sleep for this house again! Wetin be all this nonsense!*

Bimbo. Who are you? Who are you that dares disturb the holy sanctuary of the Lord? *(Running around the room; energetically)* Run away! Run away! Lest the wrath of the almighty fall upon you! Run away! Lest the sword of Angel Gabriel cleave your skull in two! Run away! Lest your children grow up ignorant of who their father is, lest …

Bimbo breaks off mid-sentence as Tarasco, a huge man by all standards, enters.

Tarasco. *Who dey curse me and my family?*

Everyone cowers and points to Bimbo. Tarasco rushes towards Bimbo as light fades, and we hear Bimbo yelping in pain.

Bimbo. *Yeh! Tarasco abeg now! Na joke I dey joke! Una no go help me! Yeaah! I don die!*

Black

Scene II

The same apartment. Bimbo, Emeka, and Lateef are seen crouching over the centre table, drinking garri from a big plastic bowl. Stella enters.

Stella. *(Contemptuously)* Lateef na only when food dey you dey wake up!

Lateef. *(With resentment)* Na you sabi. The sleep wey I sleep na my own, the body wey I take sleep am na my own, which one come be your own inside?

Stella. What are you guys eating?

Bimbo. We are eating Kellogg's Ijebu cassava flakes with H20.

There is a knock on the door, and they scramble to hide the bowl of garri. Aliyu walks in.

Emeka. Did you have to knock? We thought it was a visitor.

Aliyu. *Una dey drink garri again?*

Bimbo. *(Mimicking Aliyu) Una dey drink garri again?* As if there is something else to eat.

Aliyu. *(Confidently)* Well, all that is over now.

Stella. *(Excitedly)* What do you mean? Were you successful?

Emeka. You passed the interview?

Lateef. *The result don comot?*

Aliyu. *(To Stella)* Give me a kiss, honey. *(She obliges) (To the rest of the housemates)* Let me hear a 'Yes, we can!'

Others respond. Yes, we can!

Aliyu. *(Louder)* Let me hear a 'Yes, we can!'

85

Others respond. Yes, we can!

They crowd around Aliyu as if he is addressing a news conference. He climbs on top of the centre table.

Aliyu. Ladies and gentlemen, if there is anyone out there, anyone at all, who still doubts that Nigeria is a place where all things are possible, *Shege to you!* Who still wonders if the dreams of our founding fathers *(counting off his fingers),* Tafawa Balewa, Awolowo, Azikiwe, are alive in our time? *Waka to you!* Who still questions the power of the people? Tonight is your answer! Me! *Kai! (Excitedly)* Just look at me! *(To the others)* Oya, yes, me can!

Others respond. Yes, me can! Yes, me can! Yes, me can!

Aliyu. *Ehhmmn!* To cut a long story short. etc., etc., etc. Ladies and gentlemen, with a joyful heart, a heart long burdened with the weight of poverty, I wish to announce that I have been offered a provisional appointment by Black Gold Oil Nigeria Limited.

Cheers and catcalls drown the rest of his speech.

Aliyu. Wait! *(Silence)* I know this calls for celebration, so like a true Boy Scout, I have come fully prepared. *(He jumps down)* Here we are.

He pulls out a bottle of groundnuts; hooting and shouting follows. Emeka, Lateef, and Bimbo do a victory dance round the table, chanting a popular victory song:

> *Winner, oooh*
>
> *Winner!*
>
> *Winner, oooh*
>
> *Winner!*
>
> *Aliyu you don win oh!*
>
> *Winner!*
>
> *Pata pata you go win again ooh!*
>
> *Winner (twice)*

Stella watches initially bemused, then bangs on a saucepan to stop the racket.

Stella. *(Cynically)* Can anyone tell me what we are celebrating?

Aliyu. 'It is the answer that led those who have been told for so long, by so many, to be cynical, and fearful, and doubtful ...'

Stella. *(Angrily)* Shut up! Mallam Obama!

Bimbo. Don't be a square.

Emeka. You can be such a spoilsport, you know.

Lateef. *(Singing)*

> *Oil money is coming,*
>
> *Oil money is coming.*
>
> *No more hungry days,*
>
> *No more landlord's threat.*
>
> *Good-bye, suffering.*
>
> *Good-bye, hunger.*

The others join him, and they begin their victory dance once again.

> *Oil money is coming,*
>
> *Oil money is coming.*
>
> *No more hungry days,*
>
> *No more landlords' threats.*
>
> *Good-bye, suffering.*
>
> *Good-bye hunger.*

Stella bangs the saucepan again, and the parade reluctantly comes to a halt.

Stella. Where is this oil money coming from?

Bimbo. *(Exasperated)* This babe is daft!

Lateef. *(Helpfully)* Relax, Bimbo, let me explain this to her in simple language. *You know say Aliyu don be senior applicant for like five years.*

Stella. *Ehe!*

Aliyu. The most senior of the senior applicants in the house.

Lateef. *Those people wey him go interview for their place.*

Stella. Black Gold Oil Nigeria Limited?

Lateef. *(Cynically)* Correct! *You know book sef! Dem don finally give am the job …*

Emeka. *(Helpfully)* And don't forget that they are the highest paying …

Bimbo. And most prestigious …

Lateef. Oil-producing company in the country.

Bimbo. *(Cynically)* Is the source of our joy clear to you now, or do I need to explain it in your native Calabar?

Stella. Thanks for your concern; no need for that.

Bimbo. *(Carries on in a mockery of the language)* Okay. *Iferimpom! Mesereltim pon! Iton kom pom pom … Capice?* Okay. Celebration continues! *(Singing)*

> *Winner, oooh*
> *Winner!*

Stella. *(Going right through Bimbo's victory song)* Wait!

The others let out a groan of exasperation.

Stella. I know some people think I am daft; but if I remember correctly, what Aliyu said is that he has been offered a provisional appointment.

Lateef. *(Angrily)* Of course, that is what he said, dumb brain!

Stella. *(Sarcastically)* Oh! You mean you actually heard him mention provisional appointment?

Bimbo. *(Angrily)* Look! Appointment is appointment, whether provisional or not.

Emeka. *(A slow apprehension beginning to show on his face)* Mba mba mba! She is right, oohh! Provisional appointment is different from full and unconditional appointment.

Stella. That's my boy! *(To Aliyu)* Now do you mind telling us what makes this appointment provisional?

Aliyu. *(Confidently)* Nothing to worry about. The appointment is provisional pending the outcome of my preemployment medical examination.

Bimbo. *(Sits)* Okay, that is to say if you fail the medical examination, there is no job?

Aliyu. Sure. But I'm not going to fail the medical examination, *(Flexing his muscles)* Do I look sick to you?

Lateef and Emeka. *(Cluster around him, study him for a while)* No!

Bimbo. Celebration continues! *(Jumping up and chanting)*

> *Bi o ti e soro*
>
> *O ti wole*
>
> *Bi o ti e soro*
>
> *O ti wole*
>
> *(Others join in)*

Stella. *Stop!* *(Silence)* Aliyu, you haven't finished yet.

Lateef. *Ah! ah! Wetin be your own sef?*

Emeka. *(Concerned)* Aliyu, what was the nature of the medical examination?

Aliyu. Well, if you must know, it was the normal mumbo jumbo.

Stella. And what is this normal mumbo jumbo?

Aliyu. Chest X-ray, blood and urine test, blood pressure check, tuberculosis test, hepatitis test, physical examination, and HIV test.

Lateef. *(Pause)* Sorry, did I hear you say …

All. HIV?

Aliyu. *(Confidently)* Sure, HIV. *(Slow apprehension)* Wait a minute, you guys don't think I have the virus, do you?

Bimbo. *(Angrily)* Are you mad? Why did you subject yourself to an HIV test?

Lateef. You should have left their job for them *o jare*! Better to die without knowing than to live with the knowledge that you have AIDS.

Emeka and Stella. Point of correction, HIV.

Lateef. HIV, AIDS, they are both the same thing.

Stella. Not quite. It is the human immunodeficiency virus that brings about the condition known as AIDS.

Lateef. *(Unsure) Abeg, help me?* How is that different from what I said? *Shebi* if you contract HIV, it becomes a matter of time before you become a full-blown AIDS victim.

Stella. *(In disgust)* You are such a jerk, Lateef!

Lateef. *(Confused)* What has this got to do with me?

Stella. You tell me. Have you ever been infected by a pathogen: virus, bacteria, fungus, parasite?

Emeka. *(In mockery) This one?* As we speak now, he even has a *Lapa Lapa* infection.

Stella. Okay, Mr. *Lapa Lapa*, has anyone ever referred to you as a *Lapa Lapa* victim? Malaria victim? Poverty victim? Idiocy victim? *Eehh!* So why will you label an HIV carrier a victim? That is part of the stigmatization. HIV patients are carriers of a virus, just like all of us are carriers of several viruses, *(to Lateef)* some probably more than others.

Emeka. What most people dread is not the virus itself, but the social death suffered by people infected with the virus, death promulgated by ignoramuses like Lateef.

Lateef. *Na you be ignoramus.*

Stella. Little wonder why not one single Nigerian public figure is publicly living positively with HIV/AIDS.

Emeka. *(A slow apprehension beginning to show on his face) Na true ooh!*

Lateef. *(Obstinately)* You people should leave me alone! I am not the one that has AIDS.

Bimbo. *(Pensively)* Come to think of it, we can make money out of this.

Aliyu and Lateef. *(Interested)* How?

Bimbo. If Aliyu tests positive to the virus ...

Emeka. So what if Aliyu tests positive?

Bimbo. We can sue Black Gold Oil for violation of his fundamental human rights.

Lateef. Forget it! We can't afford a legal tussle.

Aliyu. You guys should relax. Do I look like an HIV carrier?

All of them cluster around him and study him for a while.

Stella. No one can tell just by looking. *E no dey show for face!*

Lateef. *After all Magic Johnson don get am for almost twenty years sef and you no go sabi.*

Aliyu. *(Brushing their concerns aside)* Whatever you say, but I still believe that AIDS is an elitist white man's disease dreamed up to control the excesses of a ...

Emeka. *(Going right through Aliyu's speech)* Mba! Mba! Mba! Don't be stupid. AIDS is real, AIDS is in Africa, and AIDS is with us today.

Stella. *(Sotto voce)* My brother, to be precise, *AIDS dey Lagos.*

Lateef. *(Clearing his throat)* And who knows? It could also be in this room.

Silence as they all stare at each other

Aliyu. *(Halfheartedly)* Well, it is said that man begins to die the day he is born.

Emeka. *(Pleadingly)* Mba nu. That doesn't mean you have to die the day after you are born.

Aliyu. Even if I die the day after I'm born, it's just a day out of the few I've got to live.

Lateef. Haba, Aliyu, don't be pessimistic.

Aliyu. *Ka chi walahi!* This is not about pessimism. Believe it or not, most of us will not live beyond thirty thousand days on earth.

Bimbo. *Not me ooh!* I'll live long beyond that.

Aliyu. That's what you think. Now listen, if you are lucky enough to live up to seventy years, you must have lived about twenty-five thousand five hundred and fifty days on earth.

Lateef. *(With wonder)* Are you sure of that figure?

Aliyu. You can check for yourself.

Stella. That sounds so small, twenty-five thousand five hundred and fifty days.

Aliyu. Yes, it is small. So you better make the best of the few days you have on earth. *(Giving Stella a bear hug)* Enjoy yourself!

Emeka. Even with HIV around?

Aliyu. Remember, that is still subject to confirmation.

Stella. You are a hopeless case. Denial … that is part of the problem; a lot of us are in denial.

Aliyu. Guys! Let's continue our celebration. HIV or no HIV, for now we are still alive. So, who is with me? *(Uncomfortable silence)*

Bimbo. *(Apologetically)* Aliyu, it's not as if we do not want to celebrate with you, but don't you think this celebration is a little premature?

Aliyu. *(In amazement)* What do you mean?

Emeka. Uh, uh, Aliyu, don't take it personal. Consider this. Supposing the result of the test comes out and you are certified HIV positive.

Aliyu. God forbid!

Lateef. Yes, God forbid! But suppose that happens. What next?

Aliyu. *(A bit unsure)* I never thought of that.

Bimbo. *(Helpfully)* I hear they arrest and quarantine you immediately you test positive to HIV.

Stella. (Angrily) Bimbo!

Bimbo. It's true. Do you think the government will allow an HIV victim ...

Stella. Patient!

Bimbo. Okay ... patient to roam the streets?

Lateef. That sounds true. So you mean they will arrest Aliyu immediately he gets back to that company?

Aliyu. *Na you dem go arrest!*

Lateef. *(Apologetically)* Don't take it personal.

Stella. Now, all of you should take it easy. For starters, Aliyu has not tested positive yet, so the issue of whether or not he is going to be arrested should not come up at all.

Bimbo. I know, but it's still ...

Stella. *(Continuing over Bimbo's lines)* Secondly, Mr. Know-it-all Bimbo, who ever told you that HIV carriers are arrested and quarantined?

Bimbo. *(Unsure)* It is logical.

Stella. It would have been logical if HIV is an airborne infection. However, the virus is found in sufficient quantities to infect others only in three main body fluids: blood and blood products, sexual fluids, and breast milk.

Bimbo. *(Obstinately)* All the same, Aliyu, I'll advise that you keep away from anything that will contaminate us until the outcome of your test is ascertained.

Emeka. Don't behave like an educated illiterate. If Aliyu is HIV positive, we would have contracted it long time ago. After all, we share the same shaving stick.

Silence, as they all exchange looks of fear

Lateef. Even if we have contracted it already, let us go along with Bimbo's advice until we receive the outcome of Aliyu's test.

Aliyu. *(In despair)* Hey! Hey! What is happening here?

Stella. Can I ask a question?

Emeka. Go on.

Stella. How many of you will voluntarily take an HIV test?

Lateef. God forbid!

Emeka. Ah! Not me!

Bimbo. Not in my character!

Stella. Ooh! If you are so sure that you are HIV free, why don't you guys want to take the test?

Aliyu. Don't mind them. Aliyu this, Aliyu that, yet none of you can muster the courage to take the test. You are scared, aren't you? *(Silence)* Admit it! You have made mistakes. *(Calming down)* Look at it this way: nearly every young man or woman who has had his fair share of fun has made mistakes.

Bimbo. *(Fearfully)* What type of mistakes?

Aliyu. The type that creeps into your thoughts when your mind is at rest, and your reaction is 'Shit! I shouldn't have done that' or 'God, this will be the last time, the last time! Never again, never!'

Silence

Aliyu. *(To no one in particular)* All right! So let he who is without sin cast the first stone.

Silence

Aliyu. I'm waiting.

Silence

Light fades to black.

Scene III

It's the night of the same day. Aliyu is seated, wearing a mournful look. The others are sprawled in different sleeping positions on the bed, the sofa, and the floor. Stella enters.

Stella. Aliyu, are you still up?

Aliyu. *(Clearly distressed)* Yeah.

Stella. *(Sits beside him and compassionately drapes an arm over his shoulders)* Just take it easy. It will be all right.

Aliyu. *(Rising, shrugging off Stella's arm)* Ka chi walahi! This afternoon's bravado has melted into fear.

Stella. I understand.

Aliyu. You should. After all, you are a microbiologist, *(teasingly)* even if you are an out-of-work microbiologist.

Stella. Out of work or not, I understand your fears. I mean, it is so easy to contract this thing. For us in the third world, apart from being careful, it finally boils down to luck.

Aliyu. You mean even if I am careful, I could still contract the virus?

Stella. Unfortunately, yes. In the past, many people have been infected through blood transfusion. You see, even if the blood was screened for HIV antibodies, it could have been donated and transfused during a carrier's window period.

Aliyu. Which is?

Stella. The period when the immune system has not produced enough antibodies to show up in the routinely used HIV test.

Aliyu. That easy?

Stella. That easy. That said, there still remains the most common means of contracting the disease …

Aliyu. *(Confidently, going right through her speech)* Sex.

Stella. No! Unprotected sex.

Aliyu. That is *(slight pause)* the condom.

Stella. Yes … very, very important.

Aliyu. If I test positive to this … this monster, I'll hold the government responsible. Something this bad, why have they not alerted the populace?

Stella. It's the Nigerian factor.

Aliyu. What Nigerian factor?

Stella. Okay, tell me, when did you first hear of AIDS?

Aliyu. *(Slight pause)* In the early eighties.

Stella. And what was your reaction to it?

Aliyu. Reaction? I never gave it a second thought.

Stella. Why?

Aliyu. Because I didn't believe it was real.

Stella. And it had not happened to anybody you knew.

Aliyu. That too.

Stella. So you conveniently forgot about it, right?

Aliyu. If you put it that way, yes.

Stella. You are not the only one. You see, millions of Nigerians were aware of the HIV scourge from the onset.

Aliyu. And we chose to ignore it.

Stella. Yes, it's a sociocultural reaction. Discussing sex is taboo in our culture. It is a subject we have been taught as kids to be bad, dirty, not to be discussed.

Aliyu. *(Cynically)* Yet all the adults that taught us that were busy getting 'busy' anytime they had a chance.

Stella. *(Laughing)* You know, I used to wonder, if sex was such a bad thing, where were all the newborn babies coming from?

Aliyu. I wondered that too.

Stella. Worse still, HIV was initially believed to be peculiar to homosexuals. It was then known as …

Aliyu. *(Continuing over Stella's lines)* The gay fever.

Stella. Yes, the gay fever. This gave it an even worse social stigma; however, it is now obvious that the problem is a universal fever.

Aliyu. Does it mean that AIDS has been in Africa for long?

Stella. Believe it or not, it has. Most developing countries keep poor records, and that is why the number of HIV carriers in Nigeria has remained deceptively low. But honestly, it gets worse every day. About eight thousand five hundred people contract the virus every day.

Aliyu. *(Incredulous)* You mean every year?

Stella. No, every day.

Aliyu. That is incredible!

Stella. Incredible but true.

Bimbo, who has been awake for some time, finally stirs.

Bimbo. Stella, I've been bothered about something all day; I don't know if you can throw more light on it for me.

Stella. On HIV/AIDS?

Bimbo. How did you know?

Stella. That's the topical issue today. Okay, so what is it?

Bimbo. As you all know, I've lived a close-to-celibate life.

Aliyu. *(Cynically)* Are you sure?

Bimbo. *(Waves him off)* Oooh, shut up! At least, I've only kept one girlfriend at a time.

Stella. That brings me to a point. Can I ask you a question that requires an honest-to-God answer?

Bimbo. Sure, go ahead.

Stella. How many girlfriends have you had?

Bimbo. Four.

Stella. And you had sex with all of them?

Bimbo. *(Laughing)* Of course, I did, *body no be firewood*.

Stella. Did you meet any of those girls a virgin?

Bimbo. What has that got to do with this?

Stella. It has everything to do with it. Just answer yes or no.

Bimbo. No.

Stella. I take that to mean that you did not meet any of them a virgin.

Bimbo. Yes.

Stella. Okay, so check out this scenario. You have had four girlfriends.

Bimbo. Right.

Stella. Four of them had previous boyfriends.

Bimbo. What are you trying to say?

Stella. You see, immediately you have unprotected sex with your partner, we assume that you have had unprotected sex with not only your partner, but your partner's previous partner, and the previous partner's previous partners, and those partners' previous partners … the chain is endless.

Aliyu. *(Grabbing his crotch)* Oh, my God!

Stella. Sounds terrible, but it's true.

Bimbo. All what you have said is based on one premise.

Stella. And that is?

Bimbo. Unprotected sex, right?

Stella. Right.

Bimbo. Well, you see, I started using the condom when the only brand available in the Nigerian market was Durex.

Aliyu. Smart boy.

Bimbo. On the contrary. It had nothing to do with being smart.

Stella. You mean you were not protecting yourself against HIV?

Bimbo. I didn't give the virus a second thought.

Aliyu. What prompted your decision?

Bimbo. You know, HIV is not the only STD, and then there was, of course, 'accidental discharge".

Stella. Accidental what?

Bimbo. Unwanted pregnancies. I watched my elder sister destroy a promising future with such a pregnancy.

Aliyu. Lucky you.

Bimbo. *(Hopefully)* Does this make me HIV free?

Stella. Not necessarily. That takes out body fluids like semen or virginal fluids, but leaves us with blood and breast milk.

Bimbo. *(Almost choking)* Breast milk?

Aliyu. *(Tauntingly)* Have you been eating food meant for others?

Bimbo. You mean I should not be …

Stella. Better not!

Bimbo. *(Excitedly)* I have another question.

Stella. Okay.

Bimbo. Supposing Aliyu tests positive to HIV.

Aliyu. *(Angrily)* You are mad!

Bimbo. *(Warming up)* Relax. Just supposing he is certified HIV positive, is there no way we can make money out of it?

Stella. What are you driving at?

Bimbo. *(Moves restlessly about the room, thinking out loud)* I mean, there is the World Bank HIV/AIDS Fund, AIDS CAP, UNAIDS, PATA, and so many other AIDS-awareness organizations.

Aliyu. So, what has that got to do with me?

Bimbo. *(Highly excited)* Can't you see? These organisations will be willing to dole out money if you publicly declare yourself an HIV carrier and begin to campaign for them.

Aliyu. *(With anger and resolve)* Eeeh!

Bimbo. *Walahi!* And I will be your manager.

Stella. *(In reprimand)* Bimbo, you have a criminal mind.

Bimbo. *(Beaming)* I'll take that as a compliment.

Aliyu. *(Pensively)* Well, the idea is not exactly bad, except for some basic changes.

Bimbo. That's my guy! So, what kind of changes do you advise?

Aliyu. For starters, why don't *you* test positive to HIV, and I'll gladly be your manager.

Bimbo. *(Defensively)* You are the one that has done the test …

Aliyu. And nothing stops you from doing it too.

Bimbo. I was only trying to be helpful.

Aliyu. Thanks for your concern.

Bimbo. Okay, if you don't like that plan, then we'll move to the next option.

Stella. I didn't know we had another option.

Bimbo. Of course, Option A2.

Stella. I take it that the first option was A1.

Bimbo. *(Sarcastically)* Bright girl. Now, if we can ascertain which of your girlfriends you contracted the virus from, we can sue the person for GBBH.

Stella. GBBH?

Bimbo. Grievous biological bodily harm.

Aliyu. *(Sarcastically)* You are such a bright chap.

Bimbo. I know.

Stella. But Aliyu has not ...

Bimbo. *(Continuing over Stella's lines)* I know, I know, but we are assuming the worst.

Aliyu. *(Swearing angrily) Ka chi walahi!* You are crazy!

Bimbo. Crazy? I try to get us out of this hellhole, and you call me crazy.

Stella. What you intend to do is nothing but 419!

Bimbo. And what do you know about 419? Are you a lawyer?

Stella. Well, better ask Emeka.

Bimbo. *(Mimicking a lawyer in court)* Section 419 of the criminal code, chapter 77, Laws of the Federation 1990, page 3262, states: 'Any person who by any false pretence and with intention to defraud, obtains from any other person anything capable of being stolen, or induces any other person to deliver to any other person, anything capable of being stolen, is guilty of a felony and is liable to imprisonment for three years. If the thing is of the value of a hundred naira or upwards, he is liable to imprisonment for seven years'.

Stella. You said it all.

Emeka enters.

Bimbo. The law is clear on this, Your Honour. The law says 'by any false pretence'. I repeat, 'by any false pretence'. We are not pretending here. My client here has been …

Aliyu. *(Angrily)* Who is your client?

Bimbo. I thought we had agreed in principle.

Stella. Aliyu has not tested positive to HIV yet.

Bimbo. *(Thoughtfully)* That's true. *(Slight pause)* Maybe we will have to move to Option A3 then.

Emeka. *(In exasperation)* Oh, my God! He is at it again!

Bimbo. *(Ignoring Emeka, pacing)* Supposing the result of the test comes out and you are certified positive?

Emeka. *(Exploding, angrily)* Supposing! Supposing! Supposing! When will you stop supposing?

Bimbo. *(With infinite patience)* Relax. This is a tricky one. Supposing the initial result is positive, and after subsequent tests, we discover it was all a mistake.

Stella. That is a very costly mistake.

Bimbo. *(Excitedly)* My sentiments exactly, a very costly mistake. Thereby tainting my client's name, his image, his character, and putting him through untold psychological trauma.

Emeka. *(In exasperation)* Oh, my God! And I'm supposed to be the lawyer!

Bimbo. We can sue them for damages.

Emeka. *(In bewilderment)* What damages?

Bimbo. *(Almost jumping in excitement)* Libel! Slander! If the worst comes to the worst, we will sue for defamation of character. Section 353 Laws of the Federation states …

Emeka. *(Going right through Bimbo's lines)* It's 373.

Bimbo. 353 or 373, they are all the same.

Emeka. Bimbo, you have been reading my law books again.

Bimbo. I don't deny that.

Aliyu. Bimbo, I've had enough. Leave me alone!

Bimbo. *(Defensively)* Easy, man! I didn't mean any harm; I was just trying to be helpful.

Emeka. *(Sarcastically)* Well, Aliyu clearly does not seem to need your help.

Bimbo. Okay, I think the problem is with the option I chose.

Aliyu. *(Angrily)* Bimbo!

Bimbo. *(Enthralled, oblivious to Aliyu's objections)* Option A4 is the best. That's what I call the wonder option. It deals with …

Stella. *(Angrily)* Bimbo, enough of this nonsense!

Bimbo. But I just got …

Aliyu. *(Angrily, chasing Bimbo around)* Get out! Get out! Out!

Stella. *(Calling after them)* Aliyu, wait! Please don't harm him! Emeka, do something!

Fade out as Aliyu pursues Bimbo out of the house, with Emeka and Stella in pursuit.

Black

Scene IV

Aliyu is seen drinking garri. In the background we can hear a groundnut seller hawking her wares.

Aliyu. *(Carefully inspecting his dish of garri)* Why do people always buy substandard *garium sulphate*? The granules are so hard that it distorts the capillary movement of the H2O. Can you imagine? Under standard room temperature and pressure, the L2-L1 over the coefficient of expansivity is zero. Is it because I did not apply heat, thus T2-T1 is also equal to zero? Give me NAFDAC-approved *Ijebu garri* any day.

Groundnut Seller. *(Offstage. In a singsong voice) Buy my groundnut! Sweet, sweet groundnut!! Buy my Groundnut! Sweet, sweet groundnuts!*

Aliyu. *(Through the window)* Hey! Groundnut seller! Groundnut seller! Come, come here!

She knocks on the door.

Aliyu. Come in.

Groundnut Seller. *(Curtsies)* Good afternoon, sir.

Aliyu. *(Inspecting her wares)* Good afternoon. How much is your groundnut?

Groundnut Seller. *This one na five naira, this one na ten naira?*

Aliyu. *This small thing for five naira? Oya, give me four for five naira.*

Groundnut Seller begins to carry her tray towards the exit.

Aliyu. Where do you think you are going?

Groundnut Seller. *Oga e be like say you no wan buy market.*

Aliyu. *(Angrily)* You must be stupid! Do you know who you are talking to? I have a B.Sc. in industrial chemistry. I spent five years in the university, five full years, and I majored, majored in industrial chemistry—and you dare insult me with your insolence?

Groundnut Seller. *(Apologetically)* Ah! *Oga sorry, abeg no vex. I no know say you be army major. Ah! and I think say na all army people dey enjoy.*

Aliyu. *Ehh!* What are you implying?

Groundnut Seller. *(Sarcastically) Oga you sef check am. Nine o'clock never nack, early mo mo, you dey soak garri, dey price five naira groundnut. Ah! Oga if you be major true true, na im be say some army dey suffer ohh!*

Aliyu. *(Angrily)* What! You stupid, insolent, illiterate, dirty street urchin. Get out of here! Get out! Before I break your head with this tray!

There is a knock on the door. Aliyu pauses in mid-sentence and swiftly hides his bowl of garri.

Aliyu. *(To Groundnut Seller, conspiratorially)* Shhh! You didn't see anything.

There is a loud voice at the door, calling, 'Aliyu!'

Aliyu. *(Shooing her out) Oya dey go!*

Groundnut Seller. *(Turns at the door and sniggers) Big man for mouth, no money for pocket!*

Aliyu. *(Angrily)* Get out!

She scrambles out. Enters Sammy, GQ urbane, clearly in the money.

Aliyu. Ah! Ah, Sammy! What a pleasant surprise. Come in! Come on in! *How you dey?*

Sammy. Fine, and you?

Aliyu. *(Depressed)* Don't tell me you don't know that I haven't landed a job yet?

Sammy. Don't worry, all in God's time, my friend, all in God's time. Things will look up one day.

Aliyu. Look up? When?

Sammy. Providence, my guy, providence and belief in God.

Aliyu. *(Sarcastically)* I do believe in God, but can somebody please give me his telephone number?

Sammy. Don't be pessimistic.

Aliyu. Did you say pessimistic? Sammy! Sammy! In my four years of being in the outside world, I have acquired wisdom far beyond what I learnt in my five years in university.

Sammy. There you go again.

Aliyu. I remember those days in school when there was all this talk about professional courses being the ticket to financial emancipation. So a lot of us struggled to study professional courses. I had to do an extra year because I changed from chemistry to industrial chemistry, and yet here I am. *(Slight pause)* Nowhere!

Sammy. The word is perseverance and persistence.

Aliyu. Oh? Come off it; I have persevered enough. I finished with a second-class upper and you, you finished with a third-class!

Sammy. *(Beaming)* A third-class upper.

Aliyu. *(Sarcastically)* I can imagine, and you work with a bank. A third-class graduate of philosophy working in a bank?

Sammy. So, how is that my fault? The bank is owned by one of my father's friends.

Aliyu. *Before nko!* *(Sitting dejectedly)* So, what of people whose parents or parents' friends do not own banks, what of us?

Sammy. *(Expansively)* Welcome to the real world. On the university campus, we lived in a false egalitarian society. We were all equals, no matter how rich or poor your parents were. Whatever you are on campus— social club chief, secret cult chief, academic studies chief—determined your social status.

Aliyu. And I?

Sammy. You were an academic studies (hesitates)… no! Secret cult … no! Aca … I'll book you down for chief academic studies/secret cult chief. As soon as we stepped out of this false world into the real society … puuff! The mirage disappears! And people like me, who know the right people, drive the right cars, live in the right neighbourhoods … rule the day. You win some; you lose some.

Aliyu. *(Dejectedly)* Thanks for reminding me.

Sammy. Don't mention it. *(With a hint of mischief)* Meanwhile, what was that scrawny, scruffy-looking street urchin doing here?

Aliyu. *(Comprehension slowly dawning)* Come on, Sammy, the fact that I'm poor doesn't mean that I'm that hard up. I wanted to buy something.

Sammy. *(Mischievously)* Something like?

Aliyu. *(Defensively)* Groundnuts … Groundnuts, of course!

Sammy. *(Looking around)* I don't see any groundnuts here.

Aliyu. I changed my mind.

Sammy. Have it your way. Didn't mean to poke into your private affairs.

Aliyu. You don't believe me?

Sammy. Well, strange things happen these days. *(Plunks down into the sofa. Jumps up again as one of the protruding springs snags his trouser)* That brings me to why I'm here. I have bad news.

Aliyu. *(Rising)* Bad news? My guy, nothing can be worse than my present condition.

Sammy. Well, wait till you hear this. Do you remember Shakis?

Aliyu. *(Trying to remember)* Shakis, secret cult chief … the Jah Lord?

Sammy. Correct!

Aliyu. *(Apprehensively)* What about him? I hope he is not dead.

Sammy. No, but he is close to it.

Aliyu. *(With rising curiosity)* Is he sick?

Sammy. Not yet, but he may soon be.

Aliyu. *Ka chi walahi!* You are confusing me. 'He is not dead but close to it'; 'He isn't sick but he may soon be.' What are you now? A witch doctor? A prophet? You can now predict when people will fall sick or die?

Sammy. *(Choosing his words carefully)* Aliyu, Shakis has tested positive to HIV.

Aliyu. *(Exploding from his seat)* This HIV again! *(Slight pause)* But what has that got to do with me?

Sammy. You remember Bosco and Jugunu?

Aliyu. Yes.

Sammy. They have both tested positive too; and in Jugunu's case, it has become full-blown AIDS.

Aliyu. AIDS as in *(slight pause; apprehensively)* AIDS!

Sammy. *(Nodding in affirmation)* AIDS as in acquired immune deficiency syndrome.

Aliyu. *(In fear)* My God, what is happening?

Sammy. I honestly don't know.

Aliyu. You are holding back on me. What is going on here?

Sammy. I knew you'd see the connection.

Aliyu. I might be poor, but I am not daft.

Sammy. Jugunu, Bosco, Shakis, you, and I were initiated into the Jah Lords Confraternity on the same day. *(Pause)*

Aliyu. Go on.

Sammy. On that day, we cut our thumbs with the rastaman's blade and thumbprinted on the effigy of Jah Rastafari, Haile Selaise, as the creed of Jah Lords demands.

Aliyu. Tell me something I don't know.

Sammy. Doctors are working on the hypothesis that …

Aliyu. *(Rushes at Sammy. Grabs his collar)* Doctors? What have doctors got to do with this?

Sammy. *(Explodes in exasperation, fear)* A connection, they are looking for a connection, Aliyu! Can't you see? Out of five of us who were initiated on the same day, three have tested positive to HIV!

Aliyu. You mean … *(pauses in fear)*

Sammy. *(Nodding in affirmation)* Yes, that is what I mean. One of us must have been HIV positive then, and that one must have infected others.

Aliyu. Oh, my God! *(Sits dejectedly)* I just took an HIV test.

Sammy. *(Going to Aliyu)* Pull yourself together. It is not all bad news, as we still stand a chance.

Aliyu. *(With hope)* We still stand a chance? How?

Sammy. The doctors strongly believe that Jugunu was the one who infected the others.

Aliyu. So?

Sammy. So, depending on the sequence of our thumbprinting, we may not be infected after all.

Aliyu. You mean our lives hang in balance over something as stupid as the sequence of our initiation?

Sammy. Stupid but true. Can you remember what happened that night?

Aliyu. That night? *(Pause)* I was scared out of my wits. How am I to remember?

Sammy. *(They both break away in opposite directions. In frustration)* Damn!

Aliyu. Dammit!

Silence as they are both lost in thought.

Aliyu. *(Finally)* I think you should go for the test. That's your only road to sanity.

Sammy. And what of you?

Aliyu. I told you before; I have taken one as part of a preemployment medical test.

Sammy. Forget it!

Aliyu. *(Looks at Sammy quizzically)* You are scared?

Sammy. *(Vehemently)* Me! Take that test? No way!

Aliyu. Welcome to the real world. Come on, you are supposed to be a Jah Lord, and Jah Lords don't scare easily.

Sammy. Jah Lord, my foot!

Aliyu. *(Getting angry)* Listen up, my friend! Since we left school, you have been enjoying yourself, eating the best of food, drinking the best of wines …

Sammy. *(Going right through Aliyu's speech)* What has that got to do with what we are discussing?

Aliyu. All this while, it never occurred to you to visit me. Now you have a problem …

Sammy. *(Continuing over Aliyu's lines) We* have a problem.

Aliyu. Did I hear you say 'we'? Sammy, this is your problem. I told you, I have taken the test.

Sammy. Don't tell me you are jealous.

Aliyu. Me? No way. I don't grudge you anything, but you have to do the test. I said it before—it's your only way to sanity.

Sammy. *(Vehemently)* Forget it.

Aliyu. *(Angrily)* All right. *(Pointing to the door)* If you don't want to listen to me, you may as well leave now.

Sammy. *(In shock)* What?

Aliyu. Yes, leave! Or take a look around you. Does this look like where you'd like to live? Sammy, leave me alone! Leave me to my suffering! You can do the test if you like; and if not, you can hang!

Sammy. *(Obstinately)* I refuse to do the test. I'll live out my life, and when I'm ready, I'll die after a brief illness.

Aliyu. *(Now pleading)* Think of the hazard you pose to others; think of all those young girls.

Sammy. What about them?

Aliyu. With all your wealth, they are attracted to you like insects to nectar … poisonous nectar. Do you really want to endanger another person's life?

Sammy. *(Angrily)* Now you ask. Why didn't anybody tell Jugunu before he endangered my life? Where were they then? Forget it! Do your thing, and let me do my thing.

Aliyu. *(Resignedly)* Sammy, you leave me with no choice. You have to take that test.

Sammy. Otherwise …

Aliyu. Otherwise I'll inform the health authorities. I'll leak this story to the press.

Sammy. They will get to you too.

Aliyu. *(Amused)* Me? I am not a celebrity. I can't sell their tabloids. Your father is a billionaire; they will be more interested in you.

Sammy. Are we not both Jah Lords? Why are you doing this to me?

Aliyu. Brother, you leave me with no choice.

Sammy. *(Angrily)* If you try this, I'll sue your ass. I'll sue you for every goddam kobo you have.

Aliyu. Suit yourself, but note that I have nothing.

Sammy. Then I'll sue you for every goddam kobo you'll ever earn!

Aliyu. Have it your way then. We'll meet in court.

Sammy. *(In amazement, almost pity)* You can't afford a legal battle, and you know it.

Aliyu. *(Confidently)* Don't bet on it. I have a lawyer living right here.

Sammy. *(In amazement)* He lives here? *(Breaking into laughter)* That doesn't sound like a successful lawyer to me.

Aliyu. *(Angrily)* He would have been successful if he had been given a chance.

Sammy. *(Barely holding back his laughter)* So he is not practicing?

Aliyu. How can he be practicing when people like you have deprived him of his rightful place in society?

There is a knock on the door.

Aliyu. Come in.

Stella enters.

Sammy. Hello.

Stella. Hi. *(Stumbling upon the bowl of garri)* Who left this here?

Aliyu. *(Defensively)* Oh! It's a culture dish. I'm trying to isolate the different bacteria in the room.

Sammy. What was that?

Aliyu. Oh! Nothing to bother you. Stella, meet Sammy Coker, son of Dele Coker, the shipping mogul. Sammy, this is my roommate Stella. She is an out-of-work microbiologist.

Sammy. *(Switching on the charm)* Hello! Has anyone ever told you that you are stunning?

Stella. *(Smiling coyly)* Thanks.

Aliyu. Stella, watch it! He is lethal, literally lethal.

Stella. *(Coyly)* And too fast for my liking.

Sammy. That's me, fast and straightforward.

Stella. *(Going about tidying the room)* So, what brings you here? You look out of place in these surroundings.

Sammy. *(Pause)* Well, um …

Aliyu. *(Sits down wearily, holding his head in his hands dejectedly. Urges Sammy on)* You can tell her; we keep no secrets here.

Sammy. *(Pause)* Well …

Aliyu. Go on.

Sammy. Well, you see we have a problem.

Stella. *(Looks at both of them warily)* Who are 'we'?

Sammy. Aliyu and I. *(Slight pause)* When we were in the university, we both belonged to a confraternity known as the Jah Lords.

Stella. You mean a secret cult?

Sammy. I mean a confraternity. There is a difference.

Aliyu. Confraternity, please, confraternity.

Stella. Confraternity, secret cult—both mean the same to me.

Sammy. I joined up the same time with Aliyu and three others.

Stella. Now where can all this classified information be leading to?

Aliyu. *(Explodes from his seat. Thunders)* It leads to hell with an invite. Hell's invitation, RSVP, Satan-Lucifer, number one, Doomsday Lane, Hades City, Armageddon.

Stella. *(Recoiling)* I have never seen you this worked up.

Aliyu. Worked up? That is the understatement of the century.

Stella. Aliyu, cool down. Sammy, please go on.

Aliyu. *(Brushes Sammy aside)* Let me tell her. *(Slight pause)* You see, out of the five of us who got initiated on the same day, three have tested positive to HIV, one of which has become full-blown AIDS.

Sammy. *(Continuing over Aliyu's lines)* The doctors are working on the theory that one of us infected the remaining four, that is, supposing Aliyu and I test positive.

Stella. *(Confused)* I don't understand. How could he infect you guys?

Sammy. There are two possible explanations: either we had our thumbs cut with the same unsterilized razor blade, or we thumbprinted with our cut thumbs on the same spot.

Stella. What did you thumbprint on?

Aliyu. *(Swearing) Ka chi walahi!* It's enough! She has heard enough!

Stella. You have to furnish me with enough information. Otherwise, how am I supposed to help?

Sammy. *(Pause)* We all thumbprinted on an effigy of Haile Selaise Jah Rastafari, as the creed of the Jah Lords demands.

Stella. *(In disbelief)* With your bleeding thumbs?

Sammy. With our bleeding thumbs.

Stella. How could you guys be that stupid?

Aliyu. *(Sits dejectedly with his head in his hands)* We were young, we didn't have a care in the world, and AIDS was the last thing on our minds.

Stella. Who thumbprinted first?

Aliyu. That is the million-dollar question.

Stella. You guys are up to your necks in shit.

Sammy. Are you telling me?

All are lost in thought.

Sammy. *(Hopefully)* Come to think of it, this thing happened some nine years back. In all of the nine years, I have never fallen sick.

Aliyu. Are you serious?

Sammy. Sure. Aside from the occasional malaria fever, I've been in pretty good health.

Stella. That doesn't mean a thing. If you did contract the virus, you can be in very good health for more than ten years, depending on your body's immune system. However, and more important, the sooner HIV is diagnosed and treated, the less likely it will be passed on.

Aliyu. I have been told that most Nigerians living with HIV do not know their HIV status, and those who do know are too scared of the stigma to seek treatment.

Sammy. *(In fear, pleading)* Stella, you are a microbiologist. Can't you people do something?

Stella. I am a microbiologist, not a virologist. But even at that, what could I do?

Sammy. Create a vaccine, for instance. One shot, and we are all free men.

Stella. Scientists are working day and night on how to tackle the HIV virus; but so far, hopes for a vaccine have been dashed time and time again.

Sammy. Why?

Stella. It is easy to create a vaccine if a virus is stable. HIV mutates so rapidly that individual viruses in the same patient have basic differences.

Aliyu. *(In exasperation)* I told you that thing is from hell!

Sammy. So there is no cure at all?

Stella. My dear Sammy, no virus known to man, not even the virus that causes the common cold, has a cure.

Sammy. Shit!

Stella. *(Slight pause)* Sometimes we are able to create a condition where a virus still exists but does not cause problems. That is when we are said to have a vaccine.

Aliyu. *(Excitedly)* So, why don't we do the same for HIV?

Stella. The good news is that powerful antiretroviral therapies have dramatically changed the progression time between HIV infection and the development of AIDS.

Sammy. How does that work?

Aliyu and Sammy sit listening attentively, like pupils in a classroom.

Stella. HIV destroys a certain kind of blood cell known as CD4 + T cells, or T cells.

Aliyu. *Abeg!* Layman's language. What is a T cell?

Stella. T cells are crucial to the normal function of the human immune system. In fact, loss of your T cells or your T-cell count is predictive of the development of AIDS.

Sammy. So, how does the AIDS virus manifest?

Stella. AIDS on its own is not a virus.

Aliyu. *(Getting up in exasperation)* Haba, Stella, you are confusing me.

Stella. AIDS refers to a complete breakdown of a human being's immune system.

Sammy. That is to say that your body becomes vulnerable to any infection it comes across.

Aliyu. Like my culture dish?

Stella. Correct! Like a human culture dish. So an AIDS patient may have as many as thirty different opportunistic infections.

Aliyu. *(Sits dejectedly)* Horrible!

Stella. It's nightmarish! But the good news is that there is a cocktail of drugs that attacks the HIV virus directly.

Sammy. *(Going right through her speech)* But it is not a cure?

Stella. But it is not a cure. It does not kill the virus, just stops it from completing its life cycle to become mature and infectious, in some cases, bringing the T-cell count back to normal.

Aliyu. How come we don't know much about the available treatment?

Stella. People are too scared to ask. Guys, it may interest you to know that pretest counselling is available before a voluntary HIV test is taken.

Sammy. As in *(slight pause; raises his fist in the air like a gladiator at the coliseum)* … "we who are about to die hail thee."

Stella. Not at all. It simply helps you prepare for the test and explains the implications of knowing your HIV status.

Sammy. *(Looking at her suspiciously)* I am beginning to suspect you, Stella.

Stella. Why?

Aliyu. *(Accusingly)* Yes, Stella, how come you know so much about this virus?

Stella. You know they say ignorance is bliss. Well, not for HIV. In this case, knowledge is power.

Aliyu. *(Pause. Pensively)* So, Sammy, what do you say?

Sammy. Okay. Fair enough. Advice taken. Let me consult my family … I'll be back if I still need your help … correction, I'll definitely be back. Guys, I'm off. Aliyu, I'll check on you as soon as possible. Stella, thanks for the information.

Stella. *(Beaming coyly)* Don't mention it at all.

Sammy. *(Reminiscent of their Jah Lord days)* Aliyu, remember, Jah Lords never die …

Aliyu. *(Brushing him off)* That's what we were told in that world.

Black

Scene V

Aliyu is sitting in a corner, bare-chested, brooding. Emeka is standing by the door with a roll of tissue paper, dressed solely in a pair of off-white, tight boxers, visibly tense. Stella, Lateef, and Bimbo are seated on different pieces of furniture. They pass the time playing cards.

Emeka. *(Angrily, visibly quivering)* I don't understand some people. How can a human being spend so much time in that dirty, stinking toilet? I have been waiting for over an hour!

Stella. *(Helpfully)* Knock.

Emeka. How many times will I knock? Each time I knock, I hear, '*Eeeehm! Eeeehm*'. As if to say, 'I'm still doing my thing, oooh.'

Lateef. *(Helpfully)* Then it must be Papa Uju.

Stella. Why do you say so?

Lateef. He acts like that whenever he's taking his T.T.

Bimbo. And what is T.T?

Lateef. *(With a card raised in the air)* T.T. is short for toilet time. And he comes well prepared for it, with about five or six old magazines, complete with a packet of Benson & Hedges. If he went in an hour ago and you are waiting for him, you still have a long wait ahead of you. *(Drops the card)*

Emeka. *(Incredulously)* You mean he actually smokes and reads in that toilet? How does he stand the stench?

Lateef. *(Mockingly)* You can ask him when he comes out.

Emeka. *(Angrily)* That is rubbish! It is a flagrant abuse of our fundamental rights as cotenants. After all, we pay the same rent here. Doesn't he know that his rights end where our own start? I'll have to talk to him.

Bimbo. Word of caution. Remember, he has a cutlass.

Lateef. *(Mockingly)* You had better keep quiet and stand by the door.

Emeka. Stand by the door? What for?

Lateef. You are asking me what for? If Papa Uju leaves that toilet and Mama Uju gets there before you, you will understand what for.

Stella. *(Incredulously)* You mean that Mama Uju does this T.T. as well?

Lateef. Not exactly. She paints her nails in there.

Bimbo. That is madness!

Lateef. That is not madness. It is what I call common sense.

Stella. Common sense?

Lateef. *(Card in the air)* Yes, common sense. They live with their six children in a room smaller than this one. The most private place for them happens to be the toilet. *(Drops the card)*

Emeka. Who told them it is a private place? It's a public amenity. Someone has to talk to them!

Bimbo. *Abeg* remember his cutlass!

Lateef. You better keep quiet and stay close to that door because if Mama Uju gets there before you, you may have to download your cargo somewhere less private than the toilet.

General laughter.

Aliyu. *(Walks down to forestage. Lost in thought)* It's funny, isn't it? In life, everyone seems to be waiting for something to happen. Some are waiting for death; others are waiting for birth. People like Emeka wait for someone to leave a toilet. So what happens if he downloads his cargo here? We may tease him for a day or two … okay, maybe for a year or two … and then life moves on. But for the Aliyus who await the outcome of an HIV test … that is life changing for as long as you live.

Stella. *(Walks down to him and drapes an arm around his shoulder)* Come on, cheer up, Aliyu.

Emeka. *(Teasingly)* Are you sure you are a chemist? You are beginning to sound like a philosopher.

Lateef. *(In reprimand)* Ooh, shut up! Aliyu, do you think he will come back?

Aliyu. *(Walking back to a seat)* Who?

Lateef. Sammy, of course.

Aliyu. How am I supposed to know?

Bimbo. You said you were in this Jah Lord thing together.

Aliyu. Damn Jah Lords! That bond was strong in the past and besides, this is real life, not fiction … the present … my future.

Stella. Better forget about Sammy. For all we know, he might be out of the country by now.

Bimbo. *(Pensively)* I've been thinking.

Lateef. *(Pleading)* Please stop! That's a very dangerous pastime.

Bimbo. What?

Stella. Anytime you think, you come up with one weird scam or another. I feel safer when you are not thinking.

Bimbo. *(Angrily)* If you were not my friend, I'd sue you for defamation of character.

Stella. *(Rounding on Bimbo, angrily)* Suit yourself.

Lateef. *(Breaking them up)* You guys should chill out.

Bimbo. Chill out? Were you not here when she levelled that malicious and libelous allegation against me?

Stella. I did not have water in my mouth.

Bimbo. There she goes again!

Emeka. You two should behave. You are supposed to be adults.

Bimbo. What do you mean by 'supposed to be'?

Emeka. I don't understand.

Bimbo. You don't understand? You just told this learned assembly that I, Bimbo Oluwole, am supposed to be an adult.

Emeka. I've warned you to stop reading my law books. You keep turning the law on its head. Next time I catch you reading ...

There is a knock on the door. Emeka gets the door, and Sammy enters.

Sammy. Hello, I hope I'm not disturbing anything.

Emeka. *(Warmly)* Not at all; please come in. My name is Emeka Obi, solicitor and advocate.

Sammy. *(Looking Emeka up and down)* Okay ... you are the lawyer.

Stella. Emeka, this is Sammy Coker.

Lateef. *(Realisation dawns)* The son of the shipping mugu?

Emeka. It's mogul.

Lateef. Have it your way. Mogul.

Sammy. Yes, Chief Dele Coker is my father.

Emeka. *(Launching into a sales pitch)* I'm very pleased to meet you, sir. In these trying times of global anarchy and pandemonium, one needs a reliable legal counsellor who is well versed in a mosaic of jurisprudence, natural law, and analytical and normative jurisprudence. A tested lawyer who can handle the legal aspects of ...

Papa Uju's voice is heard in the background.

Papa Uju. Mama Uju, Mama Uju, I'm through!

Emeka hurriedly takes off, leaving Sammy bewildered.

Stella. Don't mind him. He is usually like that when he is under pressure.

Sammy. *(Shrugs)* Aliyu, I have given it some thought and consulted my family. I want to go for the test now. Will you go with me?

Silence.

Bimbo. Aliyu, he is talking to you.

Aliyu. *(Sarcastically)* What for? To hold your hand while you cry?

Sammy. I have been informed of an interesting testing program. It includes voluntary counselling, testing, and a referral program. They also provide counselling on behavioural changes needed to avoid further infection or infecting others.

Aliyu. *(Sarcastically)* Another program for the rich only.

Sammy. Interestingly it is open to the general public, for free.

Aliyu. *(Slight pause)* Sammy, the truth is, this is not a burden that should be revealed to the world. I've always liked to carry my problems myself. Go and take your test and let me wait for the outcome of mine.

Stella. Aliyu, where is your usual bravado? I thought your Jah Lords act meant you'd stand by one another.

Aliyu. I know, but …

Stella. *(Continuing over Aliyu's lines)* Look at your friend. We didn't think he would come back, but he has. Right now he needs a shoulder to lean …

Aliyu. *(Angrily continuing over Stella's lines)* Okay. It's enough; I'll go.

Stella. Thank God!

Aliyu. *(Angrily)* God has nothing to do with this.

Bimbo. Aliyu, that's blasphemy. Do not use the name of the Lord in vain!

Aliyu. Look who is talking! It's the same God who created this virus that you are thanking, *abi*? Look, I'm accompanying him just to send a message. Not because of Sammy, not because of Lateef or Bimbo or Stella, and not because of God. I am doing this because I truly believe that the HIV stigma is killing me and that it kills faster than the virus. I am doing this because I believe that the true vaccine for HIV is the removal of the social stigma that scares people from knowing their HIV status and strips them of the opportunity to seek early treatment. I am doing this because I believe, I truly believe, that only when we do this will the HIV virus become as impotent as the common cold. Stella, thanks for your counsel. *(Pulls on his shirt)* Sammy, let's go.

Sammy. Wow! That was deep.

Aliyu. I said, let's go.

Sammy. Okay then. See you guys.

They both exit.

Bimbo. *(Heading for the door as well)* I'll see you guys later.

Lateef. Where are you going?

Bimbo. No definite destination.

Stella. You are not serious.

Bimbo. *(Angrily)* What do you expect me to do, stay indoors all day long and brood over AIDS? *Meen!* I think I'm going out of my mind.

Lateef. *(Getting up and packing his cards)* That makes two of us. Let's go; at least that's better than sleeping.

Bimbo. Go where?

Lateef. I thought you said no definite destination.

Bimbo. Yes.

Lateef. That sounds like a nice place to me; let's go.

There is a knock on the door.

Lateef. *(At the door)* Come in.

Charity. *(Offstage)* Please, does Stella still live here?

Lateef. Yes. Stella, you have visitors. *(Exits with Bimbo)*

Stella. Come in.

Enters Charity, Ify, and Uche, all beautiful young women in their early twenties.

Stella. *(In surprise)* What! I hope I'm safe. What brings you girls to this part of the world?

Charity. *(Hugging Stella)* Come on, love, we haven't forgotten you.

Stella. Uche, you look so lovely. *(Stroking her hair)* What did you do to your long hair?

Uche. *(Pleased with herself)* I cut it.

Stella. It looks so nice on you.

Ify. You are not looking bad either.

Stella. Oh, Ify, come off it. I know I look terrible.

Uche. If you look terrible, then I'd love to look terrible.

Stella. Uche, you know that's not true.

Charity. *(Steering Stella to a seat)* Now, ladies, to serious business. Stella, we have a job for you.

Stella. *(Excitedly)* A job, a real job?

Charity. Yes.

Stella. *(In disbelief)* You are pulling my leg.

Uche. She is serious; we are not pulling your leg.

Stella. Okay, I'm holding my breath, what's this job like?

Ify. Uche, tell her.

Uche. It's quite simple. After beating the streets of Lagos hunting for nonexistent jobs …

Ify. *(Continuing over Uche's lines)* And beating all those randy employers hunting for girls to bed …

Uche. Yeah, and that too!

Ify. *(Teasingly)* Don't tell me you forgot that. That was the main battle.

Charity. *(Impatiently)* Ladies, Stella is waiting.

Uche. Ooh, Sorry. We have decided to become entrepreneurs, run our own business. After all, we were supposed to be the hot brains in school.

Ify. Hot brains? All they want to hear is hot pants, not hot brains.

Uche. Most of them have their brains in their pants.

Charity. *(Impatiently)* Uche!

Uche. I'm sorry! Where did I stop?... Okay. Three of us have come together to form an organization known as A3.

Charity. The AIDS Awareness Activists.

Stella. You mean you are doing charity work?

Uche. That's the good part of it. We render a social service, and we get paid for it.

Stella. How?

Charity. We get subventions from local and international organizations, and from this we get paid.

Stella. *(Warily)* There are so many other HIV/AIDS awareness organizations—how are you different? What is your competitive advantage?

Uche. We do the same work, in a different way.

Stella. How?

Ify. We are taking the campaign to the streets, where it belongs.

Stella. And that has not been done before?

Charity. Complete with choreographed modern dance, stage drama, and the usual pamphlets and handbills.

Stella. *(Interestedly)* Hmm.

Ify. And who wants boring seminars and moralizing adults anyway? The youth would rather watch a D'banj or 9ice show than sit in a seminar hall no matter how interesting. *(Slight pause)* And abstinence? Okay, it's a good story, but practicality? Who doesn't like sex?

Stella. But abstinence …

Ify. *(Continuing over Stella's lines)* Stella, don't even start … we know ourselves. For me, I love sex!

Stella. So the answer is?

Ify and Uche. *Condoms!*

Charity. We need to reinforce the safe sex message. Using a condom with all new or casual partners is the safest way to ensure you do not become infected.

Ify. Always have a DDC handy.

Stella. A what?

Ify. A 'Drop-Dead Condom', more like an emergency tool.

Uche. The same way you carry a jack, a wheel spanner, a caution sign, and a fire extinguisher in your car, strictly for emergencies. We have identified two key battlegrounds, late diagnosis and stigma, and have designed carefully targeted campaigns to reduce the number of people diagnosed late.

Ify. Our philosophy is that HIV awareness should go beyond prevention and address attitudes and perceptions regarding life, sexual behaviour, and life choices.

Stella. It all sounds good to me; however, why should people listen to us?

Charity. Have you ever been to an HIV/AIDS seminar?

Stella. No.

Charity. Typically there's a dull facilitator trying to convince a pack of teenagers who are currently living our former lifestyle to play safe. We have a couple of things going for us. We are educated.

Ify. We are young and energetic.

Uche. Beautiful.

Charity. And I for one am positively living with HIV.

Stella. *(Pause. Carefully)* Come again.

Charity. You heard me. I am HIV positive … known my status for three years now and positively living a very healthy life.

Ify. *(Beaming)* You get the drift now? Beautiful, young, educated, positive—we are a walking HIV awareness billboard.

Uche. The thinking is, if we can live with HIV, then anyone can live with it … just know your status, commence treatment, condomise, and don't stigmatise.

Stella. *(Pensively)* Why didn't I think of this earlier?

Ify. Don't worry; we have done the thinking for you.

Uju. So, are you game?

Stella. Well, I'm honoured … *(hesitantly)* I'm … *(pause)* okay.

Cheers and catcalls.

Charity. There is something else.

Stella. What?

Charity. You need to know your HIV status, and that is if you do not know it already.

Stella. That is not a problem.

Emeka enters.

Emeka. Is Aliyu in? The postman just dropped a letter for him; it looks very important.

Stella. Can you make out where it's from?

Emeka. It reads 'Black Gold Oil Nigeria Limited'.

Stella. Girls, we may have yet another convert. This time, a man.

Black

Scene VI

Light comes on as Bimbo rushes in. Emeka is reading, while Stella is putting on makeup. Aliyu is reading an old newspaper.

Bimbo. *(Jumping and shouting; obviously excited)* Aliyu! Aliyu! Emeka! We've made it! It's a gold mine! We are rich! *Rich!*

He forcefully pulls Stella up and waltzes across the room.

Bimbo. *(To Emeka)* We are rich! We are rich!

Stella. *(Warily)* Now what scam have you pulled off?

Bimbo. *(Brings out an envelope with a flourish)* Open this.

Stella. *(Reads from the envelope)* Bims Ventures Nig. Ltd.

Bimbo. That's me. I mean, the company is mine and I am the company.

Stella. *(Opens the envelope)* A bank draft for just two hundred and fifty naira. Is this a joke or what?

Bimbo. It's no joke. Emeka, open this one.

He gives Emeka an envelope.

Emeka. Another bank draft?

Stella. Okay, five hundred naira. Is that why you have been shouting like a lunatic? A paltry five hundred naira?

Bimbo. *(Conspiratorially)* Supposing I tell you that there is more where those two came from.

Emeka. *(Realisation dawns)* You mean that this is not all?

Bimbo. *(Rubbing his hands together with glee)* Of course not. I have a modest estimate of about five thousand more letters like those two.

Stella. *(Adding up the numbers)* That is one million, two hundred and fity thousand naira.

Emeka. *(In awe)* One million, two hundred and fifty thousand naira? How did you do it?

Bimbo. *(Confidently)* Piece of cake, my lawyer friend, piece of cake. You know how eager people are to jump at any job opportunity these days?

Emeka. *(Knowingly)* Tell me about it.

Bimbo. *(Pacing and miming that he is reading from a job vacancy advertisement)* 'A fast-growing advertising agency in a fast-growing cosmopolitan city requires the services of a dynamic young marketing manager'.

Stella. *(Continuing the well-known script)* 'Must possess a first degree in the social sciences or humanities, with a minimum of a second-class upper'.

Bimbo. 'An MBA is an advantage, with between five to seven years work experience'.

Stella. *(Resignedly)* Not for us.

Bimbo. My sentiments exactly, not meant for us. *(Moving around the room, confidently, beaming)* So I took out my own advert. 'A fast-growing business outfit in Lagos requires the services of dynamic manager trainees. Must possess a first degree, discipline not relevant. Salary very attractive and negotiable. Apply in own handwriting and attach a current resume. *(Pauses dramatically)* To facilitate processing, kindly enclose a bank draft of two hundred and fifty naira *(waving the envelope in the air)* as a nonrefundable application fee. The draft should be made out to Bim Ventures Nigeria Limited. All applications must be received before the end of this month'. Come one, come all.

Stella. *(Accusingly)* That is stealing!

Emeka. *(Angrily)* Bimbo, I have warned you several times. You are treading dangerous waters. Sections 420 and 421 of the criminal code exhaustively deal with misrepresentation of security and cheating.

Bimbo. *(Confidently)* My guy, before they find out, it will be too late. Trust me.

Stella. So, how do you intend to cash the drafts?

Bimbo. That's easy. I have a friend at the bank.

Emeka. *(Doubtfully)* And they didn't do a KYC, a know-your-customer check?

Bimbo. I told you before, I have a friend at the bank. He knows me, and I know him. What other KYC do they want?

Stella. What of the letters, how do you collect them?

Bimbo. Simple, through our post office box.

Emeka and Bimbo. *(In disbelief)* Through our post office box!

Emeka. You must be more than stupid! How could you have used our own box?

Bimbo. Don't worry, nothing can happen.

There is a knock on the door.

Stella. Come on in.

1ˢᵗ Man. We are looking for Mr. Bimbo Oluwole.

Bimbo. *(Stepping up to the visitors)* He's not around. Can I help you?

2ⁿᵈ Man. *We get letter for am.*

Bimbo. Okay, I can receive it on his behalf.

1ˢᵗ Man. Are you related to him?

Bimbo. I'm his younger brother.

1ˢᵗ Man. You are under arrest *(flashes his identity card)*. We are police detectives from the Criminal Investigation Department, Alagbon Close. You'll have to follow us to the station since your brother is not available.

Bimbo. *Wetin I do?*

2ⁿᵈ Man. *No be your brother get P. O. Box 914 Mushin?*

Bimbo. I want to talk to my lawyer first.

1ˢᵗ Man. *Which kind Lawyer? Come on move or I'll move you!*

Emeka. *(Stepping up confidently)* Gentlemen, sorry to intrude, but this man is not accused of any crime; and even if he is, the law says he is innocent until proven guilty.

2ⁿᵈ man. *(In disbelief) Wetin be all this grammar?*

Emeka. *(Angrily)* Grammar, I am speaking grammar? You see, it is because we are in Nigeria. Seminal cases like *Miranda vs. State of Arizona* heard in the U.S. Supreme Court in 1966 recognized the rights of an accused to legal counsel, in the absence of which his rights are made known to him, including his right to remain silent until he gets a lawyer …

1ˢᵗ Man. *(Cutting right through Emeka's speech)* Shut up! *Charge and bail,* lawyer.

Emeka. What?

1ˢᵗ Man. I said shut up, or do you think you are in America?

Stella. Please, officer, I think we can settle this amicably.

2ⁿᵈ Man. *Oga* I think this man knows something about the case; let's arrest him as an accomplice.

Emeka. Arrest me? For Christ's sake, what for?

Stella. Emeka, you have said enough.

Emeka. *(Defiantly)* Arrest me, you arrest fire!

1ˢᵗ Man. *Ehh!* Okay, Corporal, show him what we do to fire. *Oya quench am!*

Corporal pounces on Emeka.

Emeka. *Oga! Sorry oh! No vex oh! Abeg I go show you the person wey you dey find.*

1ˢᵗ Man. *Stupid man, Wey am!*

Emeka. *Na im you hold so!*

2ⁿᵈ Man. So you were lying to us, eh?

Bimbo. *(Cowering) Oga I no lie, na forget I forget.*

1ˢᵗ Man. Oh, you forget your name, eh? *By the time wey I go finish with you; you go forget your mama sef... Ahh! Oga see exhibit!*

1ˢᵗ Man. *Oya, Mr. Bimbo, forward march. Corporal, leave the charge-and-bail lawyer.*

2ⁿᵈ Man. *Oga why now? Him sef na suspect and accomplice.*

1ˢᵗ Man. *If you arrest the lawyer, who will bring money to bail the suspect? Leave am jare.*

2ⁿᵈ Man. *(To Emeka) Better go find money quick quick!*

They exit.

Stella. *(Wringing her hands, concerned)* You better do something fast!

Emeka. Do I have a choice?

Emeka exits. Stella is seen pacing the room, and Aliyu enters.

Stella. I've been expecting you since morning.

Aliyu. Expecting me? I hope nothing is wrong.

Stella. Not really; I have a letter for you.

Aliyu. *(Peering at the document)* Black Gold Oil, hmm. So they have finally decided to put me out of my misery. Now let's see what they have for me.

He opens the letter and reads it. Stella watches on in silence. He finishes reading the letter, covers his face with both hands, and slumps into a chair.

Stella. Look, Aliyu, there is life after HIV.

Aliyu. *(Looking up in disbelief)* Are you out of your mind?

Stella. No, Aliyu, it's the only way you …

Aliyu. *(Rising to his feet)* What makes you think I'm HIV positive?

Stella. But you were …

Aliyu. Overjoyed!

Stella. You mean you passed the test?

Aliyu. A clean bill of health. *(Excitedly)* Stella, do you know the trauma I've been through, the mental torture, first the test and then Sammy's news? I feel as if I've lived through two lifetimes.

Stella. For a moment, I thought you had tested positive. Good news. I just took the test myself as well.

Aliyu. You did?

Stella. Yes. Some friends talked me into being part of an HIV/AIDS awareness campaign, and one of the preconditions is that we should all be aware of our HIV status. Walk the talk, if you know what I mean.

Aliyu. In view of what I have learnt over the last couple of days, that makes a whole lot of sense. That way you can encourage people to go for HIV screening and know their status.

Stella. That's the idea.

Aliyu. How can I help? Now that I have moved up in life with my new job, it's time to start giving back to society.

Stella. *(Smiling)* At least in this house, given that as of today, you are the only gainfully employed applicant, former applicant I mean, with breadwinner implications, you actually have the leverage to change things.

Aliyu. What do you think?

Stella. You tell me.

Aliyu. You really want my opinion?… I think that the real cure is that we demystify the HIV virus, and we all undertake that from this day on, there should be no stigma attached to anyone living with HIV.

Stella. That is an excellent start.

Aliyu. That is the future, my dear. That's the future of the world and the death of the virus!

Black

Scene VII

Light comes on, with Stella and Lateef seen playing cards. Emeka is reading. Bimbo as usual rushes in.

Bimbo. *(Excitedly)* This is it! This is it!

Stella. This is what?

Bimbo. This is the real McCoy! I've finally made it!

Lateef. *(In disbelief)* You did what?

Bimbo. I mean, we've made it! We are rich!

Lateef. *(In disbelief)* You are rich again? Your wealth never lasts longer than twenty-four hours.

Bimbo. *(Confidently)* This time it's for real.

Stella. I smell trouble whenever you are in your rich moods.

Bimbo. What do you mean?

Emeka opens the door and peeks outside to make sure that Bimbo is not being followed.

Bimbo. *(To Lateef and Stella)* Don't mind him. Let me give you guys the lowdown. There is a house in Victoria Island that belongs to the grandfather of my friend …

Lateef. *(Cutting through his speech)* Are you now a real estate agent?

Bimbo. *(Proud of himself)* Listen … my guy, it wasn't easy. You see, my friend's grandfather left my friend's father out of his will, so by default the house went to a distant uncle.

135

Stella. *(Resignedly)* I smell real trouble this time … *(plugging her ears with her fingers)* I am not listening anymore.

Bimbo. *(Carried away, oblivious to Stella's resentment)* See, my friend bears the same name with his grandfather, so we got hold of the title deed and altered some …

Lateef. *That is forgery ke!*

Bimbo. Call it what you want, these are desperate times.

Emeka. Sections 465 and 466 of the criminal code deal exclusively with such acts.

Bimbo. *(Angrily)* Damn you and your stupid law! *(Rounds on Emeka)* Yes, damn you! Does the law feed me? Does the law put a roof over my head? Does it clothe me? And you expect me to stick to the law? *(Thumping his chest)* I'm a hustler, and that is what I will remain. The law is an ass, and I will ride it as much as I can. Damn the law!

There is a loud banging on the door.

Emeka. *(Without opening the door)* Are you by any chance looking for one Mr. Bimbo Oluwole?

Voice from outside. *You chop winch? How you take sabi?*

Emeka. *(Bimbo tries to cover Emeka's mouth, but it's too late)* You can come and take him; he is here.

Three mean-looking thugs burst into the room.

Leader. Wey am?

Stella. *(Pleading)* Emeka!

Emeka. Leave me! *(Pointing out Bimbo)* That is him over there. *Abeg Carry go!*

Leader. *Na you sell house give my Oga Alhaji?*

Bimbo. *(Scared)* No! I mean yes.

Leader. *Oya, follow us.*

Lateef. Follow you to where?

Leader. Better cooperate or else ...

Bimbo. *No vex sir. I go follow you. Stella, abeg help me tell my mama say na so I take go for Lagos.*

Leader. *Shut up! You think say na kill we wan kill you?*

2ⁿᵈ Thug. *If to say na kill, we no go follow you talk. We go just cast you like seven bullets come find our way.*

Leader. *Na just see Alhaji wan see you. Him fit break year hand abi na ya finger, but that wan na small thing na. E go quick heal sef. Oya dey go!*

They exit with a struggling Bimbo.

Stella. *(Reproachfully)* That was bad, Emeka. How could you have done that?

Emeka. I have gone through enough trouble for him. Bimbo has to learn the hard way.

Lateef. *(Fearfully)* They will kill him.

Emeka. Not if he returns their money.

Stella. If he doesn't learn after this, he will never learn.

Emeka. Where is Aliyu?

Stella. He has gone to work.

Lateef. I thank God for him, ohh!

Emeka. We all thank God for him. Good job, great salary ... *no be poor man prayer be that ?*

Lateef. *No be for the work I dey thank God though that one good sha. Na on top this HIV thing!*

Stella. No discrimination, remember.

Lateef. *Na true ohh! No discrimination.*

Stella. Did I tell you guys that I have done my HIV screening?

Emeka. You mean you took the test?

Lateef. What for?

Emeka. And you didn't tell anyone?

Stella. Aliyu knows about it, and besides, you didn't ask me.

Lateef. *You didn't tell us? So you and Aliyu have started discriminating against us abi?*

Stella. Lateef, that's not fair.

Emeka. So?

Stella. So what?

Lateef. So, how did it go?

Stella. *(Warily)* It was okay. At least, there is life.

Emeka. Thank God, if you and Aliyu are HIV free, I begin to feel that this thing does not exist after all.

Stella. You wish! HIV is real, my guy. Sorry guys, I have to see Charity; we have work to do.

Lateef. All right, bye.

She exits.

Emeka. *(Thoughtfully)* You know, *(slight pause)* she didn't look too happy to me.

Lateef. You noticed too?

Emeka. Of course. She put up a brave face, but I have a feeling that something is terribly wrong.

Lateef. *(In disbelief)* You don't think she contracted the virus?

Emeka. I didn't say that. Besides, Stella is too smart to have HIV.

Charity, Uju, and Ify enter.

Charity. *(Sounding worried)* Where is Stella?

Lateef. She has gone to your place. She said she had an appointment with you.

Emeka. You should have met her on the way.

Ify. We did. She asked us to come and wait for her here.

Aliyu enters.

Aliyu. What is the matter? *(Puzzled, scrutinises the worried faces)* I hope all is well. Where is Stella?

Uju. She is on her way home. She asked us to wait for her.

Lateef. *(Suspiciously)* Does this have anything to do with the HIV test?

Charity. Well …

Emeka. *(Apprehensively)* Does it?

Ify. *(Avoiding a direct answer)* That question is left for Stella to answer.

Aliyu. Shit!

Emeka. *(In disbelief) Mba nu!* Aliyu, what you are thinking can't be possible. *Lai! Lai!* Impossible!

Lateef. *(In disbelief)* It's a lie!

Emeka. *(Galvanising into action; heading for the door)* We have to find her before she harms herself.

Aliyu. *(Agitated)* Yes, but where do we start looking?

Stella. *(Enters)* And why do you think I'll harm myself?

Light fades, and a spotlight highlights Stella.

Stella. Okay, so you have guessed right. I am HIV positive. So what? Has my life come to a screeching halt? Of course not. Do I suddenly feel ill, weak, tired? Suicidal? Of course not. Am I a one-man virus transmission agent? Of course not.

With the right health care and discipline, I'll probably live long, hopefully much longer than a lot of people in this room. But that again depends on one major factor, you!

Yes, my immune system is likely to weaken over time, so all the germs you carry about, all the viruses that inhabit your systems, though not a major threat to you, could be lethal to me. So, really, you are more of a problem to me than I am to you.

So why the discrimination? Look at me. Just because I have the virus, do I look less human to you? Yet you peddle myths about the virus, about me, creating more stigma, more fear.

That is the real death, my dears. The death with you sticking the dagger deep into the heart of sufferers, a social death driven by your ignorance, your haughtiness, by man's primordial instinct to feel superior, to put down a fellow man. That is the real story of HIV, and that is the key to the vaccine.

Stop stigmatization, stop discrimination, and take away the fear that strips us of the benefit of early medical care; then you will have a chronic disease, not a death sentence.

Today I'll leave you with one thought, one key thought in this process of self-appraisal. If over five million people contracted the virus last year, if this trend is allowed to continue, which is likely due to our traditional self-denial, finger-pointing, discrimination, and stigmatization, then sooner or later the have-HIVs will be in the majority, and the have-nots will be discriminated against. Think about it; food for thought.

If you stand with me today against discrimination, against stigmatization, I crave your indulgence; I'd appreciate it if you would repeat after me:

> We will not walk slowly into the dark.
>
> For the night rules only for those who will not fight.
>
> We will not lose this fight with night.
>
> For with our bare hands, we shall uproot the fright.
>
> We will not tolerate prejudice,
>
> But will bear and share the pain.
>
> We all stand firm against stigma,

For in discrimination there is no gain.
We will shine forth the light
And fully stretch forth our arms
To welcome our kin.

We will live
Together
In brotherhood,
In love,
HIV not to put asunder.
We will not discriminate
For fear of one another,
As the more we stigmatize,
The weaker our resistance.

We hold in our collective hands
The one shot that will win this war,
The real vaccine.

This day we all decree
That we will live
Together.
We will love
One another.
This … this will be the new creed
By which we will live.
That is the vaccine!

Black

THE END

This Time Tomorrow

Characters

Professor

Folake

Keji

Jide/Director

1st, 2nd, 3rd, 4th, and 5th Actors, and other (nonspeaking) actors

Stage Manager

Business Manager

Ben

Femi

1st, 2nd, and 3rd Reporters, and other journalists

Chris

Alhaji

Suru

Iya Mulika

1st and 2nd Thugs

Chief Yagba

Vincent Badmus

Scene I

The play is set in 1990s Lagos, Nigeria. In a well-furnished sitting room, a door leads to the kitchen downstage left, while a staircase leads up to two rooms facing the audience. The orchestra pit serves as the driveway to the house, and some action takes place here.

The play opens with the room, including the flight of stairs, covered with men and women, all singing and chanting, raising a racket. Professor (a hawkish, balding, bespectacled man in his mid-fifties, with an intellectual air, wearing an old housecoat and Bunny, fluffy slippers) emerges at the top of the staircase brandishing a double-barrel firearm.

Professor. *(Hooting cowboy-style and brandishing his firearm)* Yeeeha!

The singing and chanting cease immediately, and everyone scampers for cover.

Folake, Professor's wife (mid-fifties, beautiful woman, with a confident, matronly air, dressed in Iro and Buba), brings Professor under control and calms the scared demonstrators.

Folake. Professor, please! They mean no harm.

Professor. *(Peering from beneath his glasses)* Really? *(Sheepishly, sulking)* I thought we were under attack.

Folake. *(Apologising to the demonstrators, descending the staircase)* I'm really sorry for this mix-up. Professor and I want to assure you that this little problem will be settled amicably; there is no need for violence.

The demonstrators regain their fervour, and chants of 'we no go gree' rend the air. The chants die down as Keji (beautiful, mid-twenties, with an air of confidence) enters dressed for work, in a smart pantsuit and carrying a designer briefcase. The earlier chanting is replaced by catcalls and whistles from the men in the mob.

145

Keji. *(Catwalking down the staircase)* Please exercise patience. Jide will be back anytime now, and this whole thing will be sorted out. For the time being, if there is anything I can do for you, do not hesitate to ask.

One of the men eagerly moves towards her in an exaggerated swagger, and the women amongst them begin to boo him, some shouting 'sellout, sellout'. A car horn hoots outside repeatedly.

Keji. *(With a wave of a well-manicured hand)* Sorry, guys, I really have to run, as I have a meeting at the office at nine o'clock. *(Turning to Professor)* Daddy, please let me see you outside.

She exits amidst more catcalls and whistles. Jide (late twenties, a well-built and charming man) is seen in the orchestra pit walking towards the door.

Jide. *(Checking his sister out)* Hi, baby! Off so early?

Keji. *(Hushing him up)* Ssshh!

Jide. *(Sotto voce)* What's the matter?

Professor. *(Agitatedly)* Your entire theatre group is in there.

Jide. *(Confidently, heading for the door)* I'll go in and see them.

Professor. *(Stopping him)* If they are still in the state I met them, they'll tear you to pieces as soon as you walk in.

Jide. *(Hesitantly, unsure)* That bad?

Keji. My dear, they are in a militant mood.

Professor. *(Looking straight up, enthralled, as if reminiscing)* Haven't you read Yeats's *The Second Coming*?

Jide and Keji. *(In exasperation)* Ooh, God! Not one of your poems again.

Professor. *(Shocked)* You mean that you did not read Yeats? No wonder the standard of education is falling. I quote:

> *Turning and turning in a widening gyre*
> *The falcon cannot hear the falconer.*
> *Things fall apart; the centre cannot hold;*
> *Mere anarchy is loosed upon the world,*

The blood-dimmed tide is loosed, and everywhere

The ceremony of innocence is drowned.

Before he is through with the recitation, both Jide and Keji exit, leaving Professor in his reverie. Jide enters the sitting room to an uproar.

1st Actor. Director, we want our money!

Jide. What money?

2nd Actor. The money we made from our last production.

Jide. (*Defensively*) Wait a minute! Didn't I pay you all?

3rd Actor. A thousand naira for one month of rehearsals? *Haba!* Director, that is swindling!

2nd Actor. It is '419'!

Jide. (*Condescendingly, trying to steer them to the door*) All right, all right! I have heard your complaints. Ladies and gentlemen, please go home. I assure you that your grievances will be discussed in full with my production crew.

1st Actor. *Na lie!* We are not leaving this place until our money is paid.

At this point, cries of 'We want our money', 'Pay us now', and 'Monkey dey work, baboon dey chop' fill the air until all the cries merge into one chant.

Actors. (*Chanting*)

> *We no go gree ooh!*
>
> *We no go gree!*
>
> *De Director we no go gree!*
>
> *We no go gree ooh!*
>
> *We no go gree*
>
> *De Director we want our money!*

Jide. (*Shouting over the noise*) All right, all right! I have a confession to make.

1st Actor. (*Angrily*) *Better confess very well.*

Jide. I admit that some people have been underpaid, so I'm going to rectify that right away. Stage Manager!

Stage Manager. *(Slowly detaches himself from the angry mob)* Yes, Director. *(Stands by Jide)*

Jide. How much did we spend on this production?

Stage Manager. We spent eighty thousand naira on the renting of the theatre, twenty thousand naira on publicity, and another twenty thousand naira on the production proper.

Jide. *(Arms crossed, wearing a knowing smile)* That gives us a grand total of?

Stage Manager. A hundred and twenty thousand naira.

Jide. Where is my business manager?

Business Manager. I'm here, Director. *(Slowly detaches herself from the mob as well and flanks Jide; Stage Manager and Business Manager form an unconscious protective shield.)*

Jide. How much did we make from the box office?

Business Manager. We made a hundred and forty thousand naira, sir.

Jide. *(Leadingly, like a trial lawyer)* You mean a hundred and forty thousand naira for every day we ran?

Business Manager. No, I mean for the entire week.

Jide. You mean after spending a hundred and twenty thousand on this production, we realized only a hundred and forty thousand naira?

Business Manager. Yes, Director.

Jide. Giving us a margin of?

Business Manager. Twenty thousand naira.

Jide. Stage Manager, please refresh my memory. Our entire cast and crew strength stands at …?

Stage Manager. Twenty-man cast and crew.

Jide. And I paid each one of you a thousand naira?

Stage Manager. Yes, sir.

By now the erstwhile hostile actors are feeling less than militant.

Jide. And how much does a thousand naira times twenty amount to?

Stage Manager. Twenty thousand naira.

Jide. Hmm. Twenty thousand naira? Business Manager, are you telling me that after spending one hundred and twenty thousand naira on the production, we still paid out twenty thousand naira as artiste fees?

Business Manager. Yes, Director.

Jide. If my arithmetic is correct, I think we have exhausted the money we raised. Or does anybody think otherwise?

Silence.

Jide. All right! If you don't understand the complex arithmetic we went through, I'll break it down for you.

1ˢᵗ Actor. Director, we did not know.

Jide. *(Going right through his speech)* Hey! Hold on! If you remove 140,000 oranges from 140,000 oranges, how many oranges will you have left?

There is an uneasy silence from the actors (in sharp contrast to their earlier agitation), followed by uneasy murmuring and shuffling of feet.

Jide. *(Angrily)* I ask again, how many oranges will you have left?

A few voices. *(Grudgingly)* No oranges.

Jide. *(Aggressively, loudly)* I can't hear you!

More voices. *No oranges.*

Jide. *(Shouting) I can't hear you!*

Everybody. *No oranges, Director!*

Jide. *(Content)* Better! Now, I promised you at the beginning of this arithmetic class that I'd ensure that whoever has been underpaid or not paid at all will be remunerated immediately.

Stage Manager. *(Contritely)* Director, it's no …

Jide. *(Continuing over Stage Manager's lines)* Come on, hear me out, okay? We have a twenty-man cast, right?

Stage Manager. Yes, sir.

Jide. Has it occurred to anyone that Director did not get paid?

3ʳᵈ Actor. *(Contritely) Na true ooh!*

4ᵗʰ Actor. You see, you have been accusing him wrongly.

5ᵗʰ Actor. *Shebi I tell una say director no fit chop our money?*

Suddenly happy chants of 'De Director' rend the air.

Jide. *(Acknowledging the cheers)* All right, all right! Thank God this is over; and please, you guys should always remember the three cardinal rules of the theatre. Can anyone remind me what rule number one is? (Pauses expectantly)

Everybody. *(Chanting like schoolchildren)* Director is always right!

Jide. Rule number two …

Everybody. Director is always right!

Jide. Rule number three …

Everybody. In the event of Director being wrong, refer to rule numbers one and two.

Jide. *(Dismissively)* All right, folks, my call time tomorrow is 2:00 p.m., okay? *(Slight pause)* Hey! Wait a minute! Next time you have any grievances, you don't need to come and harass my parents—talk to me first. Let's play it by Vegas rules. 'Whatever happens in Vegas, stays in Vegas'. See you by two tomorrow.

Actors exit, chatting animatedly.

Professor. *(Walking up to Jide, clapping)* You are a maverick! How did you do that? One minute they were all hostile; the next, you had them eating from your hand.

Jide. *(Proudly)* That's why I'm Director.

Professor. Jide, you never cease to amaze me. So, you actually don't get paid for all that work?

Jide. *(Knowingly)* Of course I do; nothing comes for free in Nigeria.

Folake. Then where do you get paid from?

Jide. Proceeds of the production, of course.

Professor. But I thought you said ...

Folake. You mean ...?

Jide. *(Conspiratorially)* Well, that's why I'm Director.

Black

Scene II

Keji is seen in the sitting room (dressed in jeans and a tight-fitting T-shirt, checking her makeup), while Folake, dressed in Iro and Buba, is descending the staircase.

Keji. Mummy, where are you going?

Folake. (*Accusingly*) Your cousin Jane just delivered a bouncing baby boy.

Keji. (*Ignoring Folake's undertone*) Ooh, I'm so happy for her. Make sure you extend my greetings to her mum.

Folake. (*Heaves a sigh*) Keji … (*Leads Keji to a seat*)

Keji. (*Defensively*) I know, I know, whenever someone we know has a baby, your maternal instincts go into overdrive.

Folake. Keji, it's not as if I want to run your life …

Keji. You are already doing that.

Folake. You have to think of settling down.

Keji. (*Angrily; getting up*) Jide is two years older than me; why don't you tell him to settle down?

Folake. (*Standing up from the seat*) Jide is a man. He can get married whenever he wants.

Keji. (*Sarcastically*) Then maybe you should place an advert outside: 'Husband wanted, apply within'. (*Slight pause*) Mummy, relax, I'll get married whenever I want to.

Folake. (*Knowingly*) No, you can't, your biological clock is ticking away. For your information, I had you when I was twenty-one.

Keji. (*Defensively*) You were not a career woman.

Folake. But I've always had lofty ambitions for my family and me.

Keji. Mummy, I don't like this. Whenever you sound this way, you make me feel guilty.

Folake. Get me right, Keji. I'm not telling you to go and do what you don't want to do, something drastic or even downright desperate. All I'm trying to point out is that you don't have time on your side.

Keji. Thanks for the reminder.

Folake. (*Pauses dramatically*) What's your name?

Keji. I don't understand your question. What do you mean?

Folake. I mean what I asked: what is your name?

Keji. (*Baffled*) Keji.

Folake. I mean the full name.

Keji. Morenikeji.

Folake. (*Leading her back to the seat*) Do you know what that means?

Keji. Translated roughly, yes.

Folake. I always wanted a daughter, a partner; then I had you. Your name roughly translates to 'Now I have made a partner'.

Keji. Mummy, you are getting unnecessarily worked up.

Folake. I wanted to teach you things my mother never taught me, to show you the pitfalls that I fell into.

Keji. Now you *are* worked up.

Folake. I made several minor mistakes when I was young. I didn't learn, never thought life could be any worse, and then I made one big mistake. My mother didn't guide me; rather, she allowed her selfish interests to override her maternal instincts.

Keji. Mummy, don't you think it'll be good for me to make my own mistakes?

Folake. My dear, there are some mistakes you'll have to live with all your life.

Keji. Like?

Folake. Like … (*Pause*) Don't bother. You wouldn't want to know.

There is a knock on the door.

Keji. That's my date. *(Opens the door)*

Ben. May I come in?

Keji. Of course, you can.

Ben enters, a dashing young man, dressed in the Yoruba native aso oke, complete with the fila cap.

Keji. (*Stares at him in horror, eyes almost popping out; sarcastically*) You are right on time, and waooh! Do you look super! Oh, sorry, mum, this is Ben. He is one of our company's contractors.

Ben. (*Greeting in Yoruba*) E ka le ma. (*Prostrating; smiling sheepishly*) A small-time contractor, if I may add.

Folake. (*Ushering him to a chair*) You must be making a pile of money from there.

Ben. Nothing much really, a little here, a little there, I get along.

Keji. (*Quizzically*) Ben, how come I did not hear you drive up?

Ben. I came with a cab. I alighted at the gate and walked down.

Keji. Your car is faulty?

Ben. Actually, I don't own a car (*slight pause*) yet.

Keji. (*In utter disbelief*) You don't have a car? (*Pause*) You mean you don't have a car? (*Holding out both hands as if gripping a steering wheel*) In Lagos? How do you cope with your business?

Ben. *(Flustered, hesitantly)* I borrow my father's car sometimes.

Folake. *(Coming to his rescue)* That he doesn't have a car now doesn't mean he will not buy one in the future.

Keji. I did not mean it that way.

Ben. You don't have to apologise.

Keji. Anyway, in this age of the Internet, you really don't need to be moving around that much. That reminds me, let me have your e-mail address.

Ben. It's P. O. Box 50645, South-West Ikoyi …

Keji. Oh, sorry! I don't mean your postal address; I mean your e-mail address.

Ben. Uh … e-mail?

Keji. Yeah. Electronic mail. *(Pause, realisation dawning slowly)* You mean you don't have access to the Internet? Christ! You must really find it hard doing business.

Ben. *(Completely flustered; stammering)* Um … well … actually …

Folake. Keji, stop harassing the poor boy! Can't you see that you are making him uncomfortable?

Enter Professor and Femi. Femi is quite handsome, appears to be in his late twenties, urbane, and dressed in a well-cut, fitted pair of trousers and shirt.

Professor. *(Excitedly)* Is everyone at home?

Folake. I hope there is no problem.

Professor. No, darling *(kissing her on the cheek)*. I have an important announcement to make.

Keji. *(Feigning excitement on his behalf)* Let me guess, you have been made the vice-chancellor.

Professor. No.

Folake. *(Teasingly)* You have married another wife.

Professor. *(In mock horror)* Of course not! You know me better than that. All right, all right, I'll save you the agony. I have decided to run for the senate.

Folake. (*Confused*) But you are already a member of the university senate.

Professor. (*Enthusiastically*) Not *that* senate, my dear. I mean the national senate. Oh! I almost forgot. This is Mr. Femi Aluko. He is the son of my late friend, the maverick politician, Chief Aluko. Femi has offered to be my campaign manager. He handled his father's political campaigns when he was alive.

Ben. *(Seeing an opportunity to contribute to a discussion without being derided)* Which party do you belong to, sir?

Professor. The Nigerian Action Party.

Ben. (*Helpfully*) That is to say that you'll be running against Chief Yagba in the primaries.

Folake. (*In shock*) Which Chief Yagba?

Ben. The former minister for mines and steel.

Folake. (*Shaking her head*) Oh, my God! Not again, please not again. (*Slumps*)

Ben. (*Sheepishly*) Was it anything I said?

Black

Scene III

A press conference is in session in the sitting room. The journalists all seem bored, while Professor, Femi, and Jide are seen trying hard to make it work.

Professor. *(Moving around the room energetically)* The other day, I was strolling leisurely down the campus boulevard, and an inner voice whispered to me, *(pauses in mid-stride)* 'Professor'. I call myself Professor, you know. *(Chuckles)* It said, 'Professor, wouldn't it be wonderful if we had a recreation centre situated here?' Yes! A recreation centre! I'm sure you know where I'm talking about *(pointing for emphasis, nodding to himself)*, slightly after the street corner Jango, the madman, has turned into his permanent place of abode. In any case, when I'm voted into the senate, I'll help pass a law that ensures that all mentally challenged men are taken to an asylum where they'll be sufficiently and properly taken care of by qualified experts. Opposite the recreation centre, we'll have park benches installed, complete with flowers and trees so that after the day's work, the young and old alike can come and relax. Who knows? We might even have a fountain there. *(Pauses expectantly for an ovation. Only Femi and Jide applaud.)*

Femi. *(Leadingly)* Sir, what plans do you have for the real sector? I mean our local manufacturing industries.

Professor. *(Beaming appreciatively at Femi)* That's a beautiful question, gentleman. You see, for industries I have a blueprint for a central business district and an export free processing zone in this senatorial district. Of course, do not forget my dream: a cocoa processing plant to be situated smack in the middle of the export free processing zone. As soon as I am voted into the senate, I'll ensure that the appropriate laws are in place. This done, I and my foreign partners will swing into action immediately. *(Pauses expectantly again for an ovation. Yet again, only Femi and Jide applaud.)* *(Getting noticeably frustrated)* Questions? *(Silence)* Any more questions?

Jide. (*Leadingly*) Sir, in view of the falling standard of education in Nigeria, what plans do you have to address the decline?

Professor. (*Beaming, appearing to regain his confidence*) That's a very good question, my boy! Very good question! Francis Bacon once said, 'Reading maketh a full man, conference a ready man, and writing an exact man'. This great visionary was talking about the three pillars of education: reading, writing, and learning. My plan goes thus: every ward within our senatorial district will have a library. I will ensure that the entire senatorial district is flooded with books. Our children will have books in their classrooms, books in their bedrooms, even books in their toilets. Remember, if you think education is expensive, try ignorance. (*Femi and Jide applaud.*) Next question!

The journalists all look on disinterestedly. Some have actually nodded off.

Professor. Any questions? (*Silence*) Any questions? (*Sounding exasperated*) You mean you don't have any questions?

1ˢᵗ Reporter. (*Cynically*) Sir, I understand that you want to build schools, industries, parks, and what have you.

Professor. (*Enthusiastically*) Yes, of course, I believe I mentioned all that in my speech earlier.

1ˢᵗ Reporter. Well, you see, sir, you have to appreciate that such grandiose plans are the least of our worries at the moment. We all came here at great cost to ourselves, literally walked to this place given the fuel scarcity. We still have to go back at great cost to ourselves to file our stories about you, for you.

Femi. (*Almost exploding from his seat*) All that has been taken care of. Professor has made available an honorarium for all of you. Mind you, it is not a bribe, for Professor is very ethical; it is, I repeat, an honorarium. Here you are. (*Handing out small, sealed, brown envelopes. This elicits a thunderous ovation from the journalists.*)

2ⁿᵈ Reporter. (*Clutching his envelope*) Professor, that was a wonderful speech you made back there. I'll file my report as soon as I get to the office.

3ʳᵈ Reporter. Best of luck, Professor, the next 'most distinguished senator of the Federal Republic of Nigeria'. I hope we will hear more from you soon. Good day, and best of luck.

All the journalists exit, chatting excitedly and patting their brown envelopes.

Femi. Excellent outing!

Professor. The speech didn't sound too good to me.

Jide. It sounded too academic.

Professor. (*Defensively*) Who told you that? It was a good speech.

Jide. I thought you wanted to hear the truth.

Professor. All right. So what you are saying is that this entire circus was a flop?

Femi. Not exactly.

Professor. What do you mean?

Femi. You saw those envelopes I gave them?

Professor. Yes.

Femi. Aside from money, they contained a prepared text of an enhanced and more Nigerian politics-friendly version of the speech you just delivered. All the journalists have to do is edit and place it in their papers.

Professor. (*Applauding*) Bravo! That was good thinking.

Jide. It is called experience.

Femi. (*Fearfully*) Chief Yagba is an old warhorse. He knows all the tricks. In fact, he invented some of them.

Professor. (*Confidently*) How many times must I tell you that Chief Yagba will not defeat me in a free and fair election?

Jide. And who is talking of a free and fair election?

Professor. (*Staring straight up in his usual reverie*) It was Franklin D. Roosevelt who said, 'The only thing we have to fear is fear itself'.

Femi. (*Accusingly*) Chief Yagba will not stop at anything to get what he wants; and remember, he generously releases funds to his campaign manager.

Professor. He is a swindler and a thief, and you know it! I am just an ordinary lecturer.

Jide. Of course, we know that. Why do you think we are worried?

Professor. I'm going to dig up all the skeletons in his dirty past. By the time I finish my exposé on him, the electorate will see him for what he is—a common thief!

Femi. As long as he puts money in their pockets, the people will vote for him. Besides, do you think you'll get away with an exposé of Chief Yagba, the great Chief Yagba?

Professor. 'Victory, victory at all costs, victory in spite of all terror, victory however long and hard the road may be, for without victory there is no survival'. You know who said that?

Femi. No.

Professor. Winston Churchill, my dear. Winston Churchill. Good will always overcome evil.

Jide. Daddy, this is no time to be quoting historical figures.

Professor. What do you know about history?

Jide. You are dealing with real people in real life. You don't 'live happily ever after' if you cross Chief Yagba.

Professor. I've told you not to worry; I'll take care of everything.

Femi. I'm worried, ooh! (*Sits down dejectedly*) Listen, I learnt that if you cross swords with Chief Yagba, you'll end up either robbed, bombed, maimed, or killed.

Professor. I've survived worse.

Jide. Not with Chief Yagba. In his case, survivors are robbed, bombed, maimed, or killed again.

Professor. (*Obstinately*) I've made up my mind. I'll meet him at the polls.

Femi. (*Shrugging*) Anyway, it's too late to change your mind.

Professor. Why do you say so?

Femi. Once Chief Yagba reads your press conference, he'll come calling.

Professor. I don't care.

Jide. You have to care because when he is through with you, he'll get to your family, your friends, your friends' friends, your *mai-guard*, even people that owe you money. Look, that man is pretty thorough.

Professor. Remember the words of Cecil Day Lewis:

> *Tell them in England, if they ask what brought us to these wars,*
>
> *To this plateau beneath the nights,*
>
> *Grave manifold of stars.*
>
> *It was not fraud or foolishness,*
>
> *Glory, revenge, or pay;*
>
> *We came because our open eyes*
>
> *Could see no other way.*

Jide. (*Sarcastically*) That was in England *abi*?

Professor. The message of poetry is universal.

Femi. (*Vehemently*) Professor, politics, especially Nigerian politics, has nothing—I repeat, absolutely nothing—to do with poetry. It's a dog-eat-dog world. The more money you have, the more votes you win.

Professor. The great Socrates once said …

Jide. (*Exasperated*) *Jesus Christ!*

Professor. (*Continuing over Jide's lines*) The great Socrates once said, 'The only punishment to the wise who refuse to rule is that they suffer the rule of idiots'.

Femi. (*Exasperated*) I am tired of your poetry, your Shakespeare, your whatever. Listen, if you intend to defeat Chief Yagba at the primaries, you better arm yourself with something more lethal than poetry and quotations!

Professor. And that is?

Femi. *Money! Ego!* Good-bye. (*Heads for the exit*)

Jide. (*Pulling him back*) Femi, where are you going?

Femi. To my house.

Jide. (*Pleading*) You can't abandon Professor. You are his campaign manager.

Femi. (*Sarcastically*) I know, but he seems to be very good at managing his campaign himself.

Professor. That is not to say that I do not need you. Did you not read Sophocles's *Oedipus Rex*?

Jide. (*Throwing his hands in the air*) There he goes again.

Professor. (*In utter amazement*) You did not! You mean you passed through our education system without reading Sophocles? Anyway, Creon, a character in Sophocles's *Oedipus Rex,* said, and I quote, 'Cast out an honest friend, and you cast out your life'.

Femi. Professor, you are simply unbelievable! What we need now is more money, not poetry.

Professor. (*Throwing his hands in the air*) Okay, Femi, what do you want me to do?

Femi. Why don't you release funds to me and leave the electioneering to Jide and I, while you stick to your poetry?

Professor. Are you suggesting that I am not a good enough politician?

Jide. On the contrary, I believe that you are too decent to be a politician.

Professor. I don't think your suggestion will work.

Femi. Well, if you don't want it my way, I'll resign as your campaign manager.

Professor. (*Capitulating*) Well, if you insist.

Femi. I do insist.

Professor. Okay.

Femi. Thank God! Let's shake hands on this. (*They shake hands.*)

Professor. That's that, but before you leave, remember the words of Edmund Burke: 'The only thing necessary for the triumph of evil in any society is that good men do nothing'.

Femi. Where do you get all that rubbish from?

Professor. What did you say?

Black

Scene IV

Folake and Professor are in the sitting room. Professor is reading a voluminous book, while Folake is clearly dressed to go out. Enter Keji and Chris (short, cocky, overly dressed in a three-piece grey suit, complete with suspenders and a bowler hat).

Keji. Hi, everybody! I'd like you to meet Chris. He is a member of our church's harvest committee.

Professor. Hi, Chris. I'm Keji's father, *(pointing)* and you see that beautiful woman over there? That's my lovely wife. Aha *(as Jide comes down the staircase),* and here comes the Steven Spielberg of the family. Jide here is a theatre director.

Jide. Hello.

Chris. Hi, everyone *(waving)*! Keji has told me so much about you guys.

Jide. *(To no one in particular)* Is there something I can snack on in this house?

Both Folake and Keji point at the kitchen. Jide grudgingly goes to the kitchen mumbling something about women and their ways.

Professor. *(Mischievously)* I hope she told you that she used to wet her bed till she was eighteen.

Keji. *(In mock horror)* Daddy!

Professor. *(Playfully)* Gotcha! Feel at home, son.

Folake. You serve on the harvest committee with Keji?

Chris. *(Tipping his hat)* Mam ...

Folake. *(Cutting him short)* Folake is okay. What can we offer you?

Chris. Thank you, mam (*tipping his hat again*). A glass of water will do. (*Gushing, clearly enamoured*) Folake, Keji is a very strong woman.

Keji goes to the kitchen to get the glass of water.

Chris. Active in church, sits on several committees, sings in the choir, serves on the usher board, attends every harvest committee meeting, loves the Lord and knows the Word—I wonder where she gets the strength from.

Folake. (*Beaming with pride*) My Keji has always been an organizer and a motivator. If it can be done, Keji will do it.

Chris. Christ! She is exceptional. One minute she is organizing women for a self-help collective; the next she is raising funds for a community cause. It's a miracle how she juggles this with her office work.

Keji. (*Enters with the glass of water*) Linear thinking, multitasking, self-reliance, structured goals, and direct action. Structure your life like that—it works like magic.

Professor. (*Looks up from his book*) You are beginning to sound like a politician yourself.

Chris. (*Interestedly*) Are you a politician, sir?

Professor. I am a professor of literature, though I have thrown my hat into the political fray.

Jide enters from the kitchen, munching on a sandwich.

Chris. The lower house?

Jide. No, the senate. Dad always goes for the top.

Professor. And you, Chris, what do you do for a living?

Chris. I'm independently engaged at the moment.

Folake. (*Encouragingly*) That sounds interesting.

Professor. What do you do exactly?

Jide. (*As he heads for the exit*) Independently engaged is a nice way of saying that he is unemployed.

Keji. *(Rounds on Jide defensively)* Don't be rude. Chris just lost his job, and he hopes to get another one before the month runs out.

Jide. *(Laughing)* Whatever you say. But seriously, and not meaning to disparage Chris, the current trend is that independently engaged young men haunt our churches, looking for working-class young women to 'claim'. It's the biggest fraud of the century, with everybody aside from the victim ending up happy. The resident pastor is happy because his singles fellowship is seen as the surefire means to securing the ever-elusive anointed husband; the independently engaged dandy is happy because he moves from zero to hero, marrying himself a reliable meal ticket, while the unlucky woman, though momentarily happy, begins a long trek on the perilous road to perdition.

Keji. Jide!

Jide. No harm meant; just had to get this off my chest.

Chris. No problem.

Jide. I've got to go. I have an all-night rehearsal.

Folake. *(Picks up Chris's glass, turns to Jide in concern)* Don't you ever rest? You just got back from a rehearsal.

Jide. Someone once told me that every morning a gazelle wakes up, it knows it must run faster than the fastest lion or it will be killed. And that every morning a lion wakes up; it knows it must outrun the slowest gazelle or it will starve to death. In this business of ours, it doesn't matter whether you are a lion or a gazelle. When the sun comes up, you'd better be running. See you guys later *(exits)*.

Chris. *(Trying very hard to impress Professor and Folake)* Is everyone in your family a workaholic? Before we came in, Keji was telling me about the new business deal that she secured for her company.

Professor. Yes, Keji really worked day and night;, she deserved the promotion she got.

Chris. *(In awe)* You got promoted?

Folake. Yes, she is now a deputy general manager.

Keji. Mummy, you are making me sound too important. Deputy general manager is just a title.

Professor. She is only trying to be modest. You brought them business worth over twenty million, and you want to make it sound trivial?

Chris. (*Impressed*) Twenty million naria?

Keji. Actually it was twenty million U.S. dollars.

Chris. (*Aside*) Jesus Christ! I didn't know I was talking to a gold mine!

Folake. (*Rises*) I have to go. Need to attend a meeting of the women's wing of our political party. (*Gesturing to Professor to leave the room*) And you, why don't you give the young ones a chance to know themselves better?

Professor. All right, all right! Chris, it was nice to finally meet you (*exits*).

Keji. (*Modestly*) Please don't mind my parents. I am only half as successful as they make me out to be, and I definitely still have a long way to go.

Chris. (*Stands, as if to match her achievement. This also fails, as Keji is obviously taller than he. He quickly sits down, whining*) You are a deputy general manager, and you think you still have a long way to go?

Keji. (*Sits by him*) Of course. Being the general manager wouldn't be a bad idea, or even the managing director.

Chris. (*Pleading*) You know what? You could help me get a job. I mean, not the seven thousand naira a month type of job, I mean the real big ones, like yours.

Keji. (*A bit offended*) I brought you here to meet my parents, not to get you a job.

Chris. Well, you didn't tell me you are such a big shot.

Keji. I am not a big shot!

Chris. Suit yourself. And to think that I knew you all this while, and I've been looking for a job.

Keji. Chris!

Chris. I'm sorry. Maybe all this talk of millions of dollars has begun to get to me.

Keji. Oh, I'm sorry.

Chris. It's all right. Let's talk about something else.

Keji. Like?

Chris. Like you, for instance. What do you like best?

Keji. My career, my work.

Chris. Hey! That's what almost got us into trouble. Why don't we discuss your hobbies.

Keji. You really want to discuss my hobbies?

Chris. Sure I do.

Keji. Then we are back to my work—that's the only hobby I have. (*Her phone rings.*) Sorry, I've got to take this call. Hello … Yes, this is Keji, how may I help you?… Have you talked to the GM?… His phone is off? No problem; I'll be there in twenty minutes … (*glances at Chris*) make that thirty minutes.

Keji. (To Chris) I'm sorry.

Chris. I know, I know! Superwoman to the rescue!

Enters Professor.

Professor. I hope I'm not disturbing anything.

Chris. No, you are not.

Keji. You can come along if you want.

Chris. Don't worry. I'll spend the rest of our date with your parents … and don't forget what I told you.

Keji. About what?

Chris. About the job … serious!

Exit Keji. The phone in the sitting room rings, and Professor dashes to pick it up.

Professor. Hello … What? Sunrise Hotel? No way! Hold on, who is this? *(The line apparently goes dead.)*

Chris. Who was that?

Professor. I have no idea.

Black

Scene V

Alhaji is sprawled on a seat in the sitting room with a newspaper over his face. Femi is seen walking towards the house. (This action takes place in the orchestra pit.) As he approaches, Suru emerges from a corner.

Suru. *Bros Femi.*

Femi pretends not to hear, feigns he has forgotten something, and makes an immediate U-turn.

Suru. *(Cornering him) Bros Femi! Bros Femi! No be you I dey call?*

Femi. Oh! Suru! *Suru de tailor!* I've been trying to get in touch with you. It appears that your phone is out of order.

Suru. *Haba Femi! You don come again. Who dash me phone?*

Femi. *(Apologetically)* Oh, sorry, Suru. For a moment, I thought you were my other tailor. His shop is located in the lobby of the Nicon Noga Hilton Hotel Abuja, right beside the Capital Bar, where all the big boys hang out. You see, he has a telephone and a fax machine, so it is very convenient for me to get in touch with him.

Suru. *(Impressed) Aah! That one na big tailor. But Bros Femi how far with that cloth I sew for you, you never pay me de money.*

Femi. Is that so? How come I forgot about it? Okay, let me give you a cheque.

Suru. *(Apologetically) Aah! Bros! I prefer cash this time. You remember say the last cheque wey you give me bounce for bank.*

Femi. *(Feigning anger)* Don't mind that *yeye* bank manager. He just wanted to embarrass me. Can you imagine the idiot wanted me to loan his bank twenty million naira?

Suru. *Aaah! That money plenty ooh!*

Femi. You can imagine, in these hard times when most banks are distressed.

Suru. *Bros, no give them ooh!*

Femi. Of course, I refused. So they resorted to harassing and embarrassing me. Any cheque I issued, they would claim it bounced. Do you know how much I have in that stupid bank of theirs?

Suru. *Bros, you know say I be small man, how I go take know?*

Femi. As of the last time I had a transaction there, I had forty million and two hundred thousand naira, eighty-two thousand U.S. dollars, and five hundred thousand pounds sterling.

Suru. *Aaah! You even get dollars and pounds there sef!*

Femi. *Before nko!* To avoid confusion, I always tell them to keep my naira in one place, my dollars in another place, and the pounds sterling in an air-conditioned bank vault so that it will not depreciate by absorption.

Suru. *(Confused)* Depreciate by absorption?

Femi. *(In mock horror)* You have never heard of osmosis? The movement of molecules from a region of higher concentration to a region of lower concentration through a semipermeable membrane? If you keep the hard currency with the naira, the naira will corrupt the hard currency by making it soft.

Suru. *(Realisation dawning)* From hard currency to soft currency?

Femi. *(Leading him on)* Yes. Because the dollars will be struggling with the naira and the naira will be fighting the pounds, there will be crisis in the vault, which will lead to a state of emergency. If this state of emergency is not addressed immediately, the money will become distressed.

Suru. *Na im dey cause distressed bank?*

Femi. *Yes ke!* That reminds me, you know I'm now the campaign manager of Professor Ogundero.

Suru. *Na so I hear.*

Femi. Well, the members of the senate will be requiring that type of *Babariga* you made for me the last time.

Suru. *Eeeh!*

Femi. Sure. I could have taken the contract to my tailor in Nicon Noga Hilton because I felt you did not have the required experience.

Suru. *Me ke! Haba! I get experience well well. I don be tailor since dem born me, I even hear say as I dey my mama belle I don dey cut and sew so tey dey born me with needle for my hand. When I small, as my mama dey cut cloth na so my papa dey sew am, me sef, I go dey put zip and buttons, den my little sister, that one, in work na to dey iron dey cloth wey dey don sew finish.*

Femi. What of working experience?

Suru. *Walking experience? Eeeh! I don try for that one sef. When I come Lagos, I don be Obioma, Ejika ni shop, for five years. Sometimes sef, I go waka from Aradagun for inside Badagry, reach Ikorodu town! Which walking experience pass that one?*

Femi. All right then; the job is yours. Meet me next week to draw-up the paperwork.

Suru. *But, eeh! Bros, what about dey money you dey owe me?*

Femi. Are you still talking about that money? Chicken feed, ordinary two thousand naira, when we are talking about a two million naira contract. Well, if you want to jeopardize your chances … (*He dips his hand in his pocket, ostensibly to give him the money.*)

Suru. *Aaah! Bros, no be so. You fit hold am till we finish the contract.*

Femi. Now you sound like a businessman.

Suru. Thank you, sir.

Femi. Don't thank me; thank God, who put me in the position to help you.

Suru. I go come next week Tuesday.

Femi. Make it Friday; I have a meeting on Tuesday.

Suru. All right, sir, *E se sir*!

Femi. I'll be expecting you. Bye.

Suru. Bye. *(In a soliloquy)* Two million naira! Two million naira! Ah! *If I get that one, I go marry this year be that.*

Femi. Good riddance. *(Enters the house)*

Folake. There is someone waiting to see you.

Femi cautiously approaches the seated man.

Femi. Hello.

Alhaji removes the newspaper covering his face.

Femi. Aaah! Alhaji, I've been expecting you.

Alhaji. *You no know my house?*

Femi. It is this politics thing, Alhaji. I hardly have time to do anything else, not even to eat.

Alhaji. *Leave that one jo! Whey my rent?*

Femi. Alhaji, try and understand. This is election season, and I've invested so much in this programme.

Alhaji. *Na you dey contest abi na Professor?*

Femi. Of course, it's Professor, but I am also financially involved. Don't worry. By this time next week, I'll bring your rent myself. If you want, I'll even help pay it into your account.

Alhaji. I don't want to hear anything! That reminds me. Nitel officials came to the house yesterday. They said you've not been paying your telephone bills.

Femi. Leave those stupid Nitel people. Alhaji, I don't know what this country is turning into. Can you imagine that they sent me a bill claiming I called somebody in Bujumbura? Alhaji, *abeg*, do you know where Bujumbura is?

Alhaji. I don't know.

Femi. You see, neither do I, yet they want me to pay the bill. Anyway, once Professor gets to the senate, I'm going to prevail on him to move for a law that will make telephone use in this country free for all.

Alhaji. Is that possible?

Femi. Of course! In this country, anything is possible.

Alhaji. That is to say, I'll be calling my son in London anytime I want?

Femi. Of course, yes. That reminds me. I have to call a friend in London. I want to nominate him to handle the contract for the new multipurpose recreation centre, but I'm still not sure if he can handle a Nigerian structure. He would be more conversant with building houses for cold climates, you know, Europe and North America;, he might have a problem with our tropical climate.

Alhaji. But I am a reputable contractor, an importer and exporter, a dealer in general merchandise. Have you forgotten?

Femi. Do you have the experience?

Alhaji. Of course I do.

Femi. Okay then. Next week bring your certificate of incorporation, evidence of tax payment, and all other relevant documents. I'll tell Professor to draw up the relevant papers right away. The job is yours.

Alhaji. Just like that?

Femi. Just like that.

Alhaji. Wait a minute. I hope this is not 419?

Femi. I beg your pardon?

Alhaji. Is Professor not just about to contest the primaries? He has not even qualified to run for the main election, much less being a senator, so how will he be able to award this contract to me?

Femi. Ooh! So you haven't heard? Professor is the party's consensus candidate. Not only that; he is the adopted choice of the powers that be. *Make you no tell anybody ooh!* There won't be an election. Professor is as good as a senator already.

Alhaji. *Eeeh!* All right then, *abeg* greet the senator for me. *Tell am say his boys dey hungry. I go bring the documents next week. Femi, don't fail me oh!*

Femi. Of course not! That's what friends are for.

Alhaji. That's true. After all, I don't disturb you for your outstanding rent, do I?

Femi. Of course, you don't!

Alhaji. If you facilitate this contract for me, you won't need to be paying me rent again.

Femi. Haba Alhaji! That's not necessary.

Alhaji. No, don't see it as a bribe. It's a token of my appreciation.

Femi. No problem then. So long as it is not a bribe.

Alhaji. Of course, it's not a bribe.

Femi. Then I'll see you next week.

Alhaji. Bye-bye!

Femi. Bye.

Alhaji exits as Femi ascends the staircase. Jide enters.

Jide. There is a woman out there asking after you. She says she is Iya …?

Femi. Iya Mulika? Tell her I'm in a meeting. No! Tell her I have gone to Abuja. Tell her I've gone to see the provisional ruling council. You can tell her anything, so long as you don't tell her that I'm in this house!

Black

Scene VI

Still the same day. Femi is sprawled on the settee, reading a newspaper. There is a knock on the door. Femi cautiously peeps through the window, but can't seem to make out the person at the door. The knocking persists.

Femi. *(Affecting a falsetto)* Who is it?

Voice. I'm looking for Mr. Femi.

Femi. And who are you?

Voice. I have a message from Chief Yagba.

Femi cautiously opens the door, and Iya Mulika barges in.

Femi. What the …?

Iya Mulika. *I don catch you today! You think say I no know say na you been dey talk?*

Femi. Hold on a minute! Where is the fellow from Chief Yagba?

Iya Mulika. *Na me, I know say you no go open the door if you hear my voice, na im I come do wetin you do (in a falsetto) I come change my voice.*

Femi. You changed your voice to gain entry into my house?

Iya Mulika. *Before nko! You wey dey hide from me, wetin you wan make I do?*

Femi. It's not as if I am hiding from you. The political climate in this country is very volatile—kidnappings, murder, arson. One needs to know who is at his door before he opens.

Iya Mulika. *All that one na grammar. As I don enter this house today, you go give me all the money wey you dey owe me today, today! (She girds her headgear around her waist, apparently spoiling for a fight.)*

Femi. Iya, there is no cause for alarm. We don't have to quarrel over this little sum of money.

Iya Mulika. *Which kin little money! If to say e little, why you never pay me my money since?*

Femi. I sincerely apologise, Iya Mulika. I've been terribly tied up. You know, this politics thing is pretty demanding. Only last night I …

Iya Mulika. *Ehh! You don start with your sweet mouth! I no wan hear anything. Just give me my money make I carry myself commot from this place!*

Femi. Please sit down. Let me get you …

Iya Mulika. *My money!*

Femi. All right. How much do I owe you?

Iya Mulika. One thousand and two hundred naira *pere!*

Femi. *Ole! Thief! When e take reach one thousand two hundred naira?*

Iya Mulika. *You no go know. When you dey do big man, how you go take sabi. Abeg give me my money joo!*

Femi. If you remember correctly, what I owe you is eight hundred and ninety five naira zero kobo.

Iya Mulika. *The one wey you dey owe Mulika nko? No be three hundred and five?*

Femi. Yes.

Iya Mulika. Oh! *You no before eh! Ole! Abi something dey worry you for head? Eight hundred and ninety five naira plus three hundred and five naira, no be one thousand two hundred naira?*

Femi. Look, don't insult me because of a common one thousand two hundred naira. I am a respectable politician, youth leader, opinion leader, and leader of thought.

Iya Mulika. (*Singing a Shina Peters tune*)

> *Grammar, grammar, grammar no be my language,*
> *Grammar, grammar, grammar no be money.*

177

Femi. Please don't make noise here! This is not a marketplace; it's a respectable residential quarter.

Iya Mulika. *(Approaches Femi menacingly) You still get mouth to talk abi?*

Femi. Hey! No! No! Let us settle this amicably. *But Iya Mulika, you sef, you no get discount for your customers?*

Iya Mulika. *Now you wan discount you no speak grammar again. Abeg, I don tire for your tory. Give me my money joo!*

Femi. Okay! Okay! If you want it that way *(puts his hand in his pocket as if reaching for money).* Meanwhile, I've been told to nominate a leader for our party's market women's wing.

Iya Mulika. *Una get market women's wing?*

Femi. Of course. Who do you think is in charge of purchasing all the salt, rice, and bales of cloth we distribute to our female supporters?

Iya Mulika. *Wetin person fit do to be the leader?*

Femi. You just have to be a marketwoman, that is all. Incidentally, I have started negotiations with Iya Dupe. She seems like a likely candidate.

Iya Mulika. *Ah! Ah! Na Iya Dupe na im you wan give am? Iya Dupe wey no sabi anybody ke!* (Thumping her chest) *Na me wey sabi people well well. You know no say if you make me leader, I fit carry dem market women come vote for you well well. Even sef, when they give me money to buy those things, I go dey give you egunje' on top.*

Femi. Unfortunately Iya Dupe has been selling her provisions to me on credit on a regular basis. But you, before I move from here to there, it's *Femi, owo mi da? Femi, owo mi da?* Well, this is business: you rub my back, I rub your back.

Iya Mulika. *Oga, you know wetin go happen? I go leave this money wey you dey owe me to show you say me sef sabi business, but you must make me leader for the market women dem wey dey your party!*

Femi. Well, I don't know. You see, I've already promised Iya Dupe that position, and I'll have to talk to some people …

Iya Mulika. *Bros Femi, na you dey talk like this? Abeg leave that woman wey no sabi anything. In fact that one thousand two hundred naira wey you dey owe me, take am settle those people wey you wan talk to.*

Femi. *Iya Mulika, na because say na you. I no dey do this kind thing ooh! Normally I no dey gree for all this backyard business.*

Iya Mulika. *Bros, abeg no vex, I go come again tomorrow make I know how far.*

Femi. I'll be going to Abuja tomorrow.

Iya Mulika. Abuja?

Femi. Of course. Don't you know that I give the provisional ruling council feedback on the state of the transition programme?

Iya Mulika. *See Femi oh! You don become big man finish!*

Femi. *Na so!* We politicians have friends in high places. Come back next week, and I'll see what I can do for you.

Iya Mulika. Thank you, sir.

Femi. Oh, don't mention it.

Iya Mulika. *No forget ooh!*

Femi. Trust me, I wouldn't forget. I'll even input your request on my palmtop computer.

Iya Mulika. *You go put my name for computer?*

Femi. Yes, I'll do that for you.

Iya Mulika. *Jesu ose ooh! Me sef I don dey big small small. My name for computer? Shey na Iya Mulika you go put inside abi make I give you my husband name?*

Femi. Don't worry, Iya Mulika will do.

Keji enters.

Keji. Hi, Femi.

Femi. You're back early.

Keji. I came to pick up some work I forgot at home.

Femi. Keji, this is Iya Mulika. She is soon to become the marketwomen's leader of our great party.

Keji. Oh! She is a member of your party too?

Femi. Not yet, but all that will be taken care of.

Keji. You are welcome, Iya. Sorry I have to hurry out. See you next time. *(Exits)*

Iya Mulika. *Na your wife be that?*

Femi. No!

Iya Mulika. *E be like say she get money?*

Femi. Yes, she does. Actually, she is a very big woman.

Iya Mulika. *Man wey marry this one no need to work again. She don get money berekete already.*

Femi. She is Professor's daughter.

Iya Mulika. *And you talk say yo no wan marry am.*

Femi. I said that she is not my wife.

Iya Mulika. *See you. You no know say as you be Professor Manager so, e fit throw you comot anytime, but if you be him son-in-law …*

Femi. Iya Mulika, what are you suggesting?

Iya Mulika. *She fine, she get money, her papa go soon be senator, you sef check am!*

Black

Scene VII

Professor is seen throwing pieces of luggage from his bedroom out the door. From his staggering gait, it is obvious that he has had more than his fair share of alcohol. Keji enters.

Keji. Daddy, what are you doing?

Professor. Woman, what does it appear that I am doing?

Keji. Are those not Mummy's things?

Professor. (*Sarcastically*) Do they look like mine?

Jide enters.

Jide. What is going on here?

Professor continues, almost leisurely flinging clothes, bags, etc. out the door.

Jide. Daddy, what is going on?

Professor. Why don't you wait and ask your mother?

Jide. No! You tell us. I believe we have a right to know! We demand to know what is going on!

Professor. Why don't you go and play football, drink beer, chase women, or do whatever it is you young men do with your time these days? This affair is between your mother and me.

Keji. We are not moving an inch till you tell us what is going on.

Professor. My dear, go and play *ten-ten* or play with your dolls. But please move out of my way, or I'll be forced to move you violently. (*Storms out*)

Jide and Keji. This is serious!

Jide. I have never seen him like this before.

Keji. What do we do now?

Jide. Let's wait it out.

Keji. Wait it out? Is that the best you can do?

Professor enters.

Professor. I know that she is the one that has been instigating you to rebel against me.

Keji. What in God's name are you talking about?

Professor. Look at them! You think you are more intelligent than me *abi*? Let me tell you: you are not! After all, you were not there when I impregnated your mother. (*Chuckles hysterically*)

Keji. I did not beg to be born!

Jide. Keji, that's enough.

Professor. No, let her talk. Go on.

Jide. Professor!

Professor. This is none of your business!

Keji. Fathering a baby is no problem. It's being a man before you become a father that is difficult.

Professor. What do you know about fatherhood? You think you are smart because you attended a university? Which I paid for, by the way. Let me tell you, you are no different from the Jide and Keji I was bouncing on my knees a few years back.

Jide. Daddy, that was not necessary.

Professor. All right! Come here both of you. Come on! I will not touch you. Sit down. So you think you are old enough to dabble in adult affairs?

Keji. There is no age limit when what is being discussed concerns one's family.

Professor. You are speaking *turenchi!* When I'm through with what I have to tell you, your lives will never be the same again. Okay ... (*mimicking the opening chant for local folklore*) story! Story! *(Silence)* Aren't you going to respond? Story! Story!

Jide. Daddy, what are you ...

Professor. I am not your daddy.

Keji. Okay, we will listen to your story, but you don't have to take it out on Jide.

Professor. I am not taking anything out on anybody. I promised to talk, and I've just given you the first instalment of the story.

Jide. What do you mean?

Professor. I mean what I said: I am not your father.

Keji. You must be joking.

Jide. Let's cut this off. He is more drunk than I thought.

Professor. Am I? You are the ones who wished to listen to adult stories.

Keji. You can't be serious.

Professor. Jide was born six months after I got married to your mummy.

Keji. Everybody knows that.

Professor. And everybody naturally assumed that I married her because I got her pregnant, right?

Keji. Right.

Professor. Wrong!

Jide. So who is my father?

Professor. *(Suddenly sober)* I'm sorry, I shouldn't have gone this far.

Jide. Too late to be sorry, old man. *(Practically pouncing on him)* So, who is my father?

Professor. Get your hands off me!

Keji. Please, take it easy! Please!

Jide. (*Thundering*) *I said, who is my father?*

Professor. (*Capitulating*) All right, all right! (*In a subdued tone*) Chief Yagba.

Keji. *What!*

Jide. You must be kidding me.

Keji. The same Chief Yagba? The billionaire?

Professor. (*Sarcastically*) Of course, he is a billionaire. When he was the minister for power and steel, his major preoccupation was stealing.

Keji. I used to wonder about your rivalry. You sound very bitter.

Professor. Of course, I am bitter. I was engaged to marry your mother when Chief Yagba came into our lives. The rest is history, and now he has scarred us for life.

Jide. (*In disbelief*) Daddy, you are kidding, aren't you?

Professor. Unfortunately not. I was all set to marry your mother. Then I was a young man, full of dreams, with a promising future. Everybody was happy for both of us.

Keji. Until Chief Yagba came.

Professor. Until Chief Yagba came. You can imagine, he came to your mother's house in a Rolls Royce Silver Cloud.

Jide. He must have been rich even then.

Professor. Yes, so you can imagine how your mother's parents felt. Her old man didn't even own a bicycle, and right there on his doorstep was the man who could change their lives forever.

Keji. But you were not bad off?

Professor. Now, yes, but not then. Then I was the promising son of the village school headmaster.

Jide. If Mummy's parents supported him, then why didn't he marry her?

Professor. He sure gave them the impression that he would. After showering Folake and her parents with gifts and money, he took her on a trip to Paris.

Keji. She has never mentioned a Paris trip.

Professor. She will not. She came back after one month a broken woman. It wasn't until the second month that she knew she was pregnant.

Keji. You mean ...

Professor. Yes, and it was the same parents who pushed her to Chief Yagba that refused to have anything to do with an abortion.

Jide. What happened in Paris?

Professor. Chief Yagba abused her. He never saw her as a woman. As far as he was concerned, she was one out of several of his beautiful toys that he could use and dispense with at will.

Keji. Like his Rolls Royce Silver Cloud?

Professor. Like his Rolls Royce Silver Cloud.

Jide. I see. So you saved Mummy from shame by marrying her.

Professor. Yes. I still took her back. I did love her; I still love her.

Keji. But I still don't get it. Are you throwing Mummy out now because of something she did years ago?

Professor. No, I'm not. Folake has gone back to Chief Yagba!

Keji. Aah! Daddy, don't be ridiculous!

Professor. I saw them with my own eyes.

Jide. I don't believe this. Mummy is too old for that kind of thing.

Professor. My dear, women are never too old for that kind of thing.

Jide. What happened?

Professor. Someone called to tell me that Folake was at the Sunrise Hotel with Chief Yagba.

Jide. Who called?

Professor. I don't know, and I don't care to know. He told me to go to the Sunrise Hotel; and just as he said, I saw Folake entering the lobby with Chief Yagba.

Jide. Daddy, how can you fall for this? This is obviously …

Folake enters.

Professor. *(Blocking her path)* Where are you coming from?

Folake. I had a meeting at the Sunrise Hotel.

Professor. *(Angrily)* With Chief Yagba *abi*?

Folake. *(Unsure)* Well, he came there as well.

Professor. *(Screaming)* Liar! Liar! You had a date with him! I saw you. Liar!

Folake. What are you talking about? What are my things doing outside?

Professor. *(Shrieking)* Answer: I threw them out. Question: What will happen to you if you don't leave my house this minute? Answer: I will blow your stupid head off. *(Storms off to his room)*

Folake. What did I do?

Keji. *(Fearfully)* He saw you at the Sunrise Hotel with Chief Yagba.

Folake. Of course, I was at the Sunrise Hotel. That was the venue for the meeting of the women's wing of our party.

Jide. Women's wing? What was Chief Yagba doing there?

Folake. He was presenting his candidacy to us. *(Realisation dawns as she stares at both of them.)* He has told you, hasn't he?

Jide. *(Coldly)* Yes.

Folake. *(Moving to embrace him)* Oh, Jide, I'm so sorry.

Jide. *(Stepping aside)* So, when were you going to tell me?

Professor enters with his gun.

Keji. *(Screaming)* Look out! He has a gun!

Professor. *(Pointing the gun at Folake)* What are you still doing here?

Jide. *(Pleading, stepping between Folake and Professor)* Daddy, wait! Let her explain!

Professor. *(Angrily)* Explain what? I've told her to leave! She can explain from her parents' house.

Jide. *(Gently)* Why don't you drop the gun first?

Professor. *(Screaming)* Get out of my way! I said, get out!

Jide grabs the gun, and they grapple, falling to the ground. A shot rings out. Folake and Keji scream.

BLACK

Scene VIII

Femi is in the sitting room putting finishing touches to placards bearing political slogans. There is a loud banging on the door. Femi opens the door, and two thugs come charging into the room.

1ˢᵗ Thug. Where is Professor? Where is the Professor?

Femi. *(Looking nonplussed)* Take it easy. Is there anything I can do for you?

2ⁿᵈ Thug. Are you Professor?

Femi. No, I'm not, but …

1ˢᵗ Thug. *(Cutting him short)* Then shut up. Where is he?

Professor enters.

Professor. *(Calmly)* What is the problem?

1ˢᵗ Thug. Chief wants to see you!

Professor. And who is this 'chief' of yours?

2ⁿᵈ Thug. The most distinguished Right Honourable Chief Yagba.

Professor. *(Calmly and turning away)* Then tell him to come and see me here.

Chief enters in grand style.

Chief. I am sorry for the intrusion, Mr. Ogundero.

Professor. *(Correcting him)* Professor Ogundero.

Chief. *(Sarcastically)* You were Mr. Ogundero the last time we met.

Professor. That was some thirty years ago.

Chief. Was it? How time flies.

Professor. *(Sarcastically)* Mr. Yagba, I'm sure you did not come here to discuss the passage of time with me.

Chief. *(Correcting him)* It's Chief Yagba.

Professor. *(Sarcastically)* How time flies. It was Mr. Yagba the last time we met.

Chief. *(Conceding)* Okay, you've made your point. Can we talk?

Professor. *(Nonplussed)* Feel free.

Chief. *(Gesturing at Femi)* This room seems to be a little too crowded.

Professor. *(Gesturing at the thugs)* You can tell your thugs to wait for you outside.

Chief. These gentlemen don't like being called names. It brings out the beast in them.

Professor. Okay. Whatever you call them …

Chief. They are my odd-job deputies.

Professor. Then tell your odd-job deputies to step outside.

Chief. Don't worry about them. I've trained them to hear only what I want them to hear.

Professor. I am not complaining; you are the one who wanted privacy.

Chief. What of that fellow over there?

Professor. He is my campaign manager.

Chief. Tell him to excuse us.

Professor. Don't worry; I've trained him to hear only what I want him to hear.

Chief. *(Conceding again)* Okay, you've made your point.

Professor. So, what do you have to say? I don't have all day.

Chief. (*Sarcastically*) Well, for starters, I'd like to commiserate with you over the little shooting incident that occurred here. I learnt your son was hurt. Mr. Ogundero …

Professor. (*Cutting through his speech*) *Professor* Ogundero.

Chief. Professor Ogundero, you really should be more careful with the way you handle firearms.

Professor. (*Angrily*) You set me up!

Chief. (*Mockingly*) Oh? Come on! How can a date with my ex-girlfriend amount to a setup?

Professor. (*Angrily*) You had no date with her, and you know it. You had someone call me, and you made sure I was at the scene as you walked into that hotel with her.

Chief. (*Applauding*) Bravo, Professor Ogundero! You were always good at figuring things out for yourself.

Femi. That was cheap!

Chief. I was at the hotel, yes! Folake was at the hotel, and so were twenty other women leaders. It's a pity that you came just as I was walking in with Folake, a real pity. The conclusion that was drawn was yours, not mine.

Femi. (*Angrily*) You are an animal!

Chief. (*Conspiratorially; laughing*) That reminds me: my deputies don't like people calling me names either.

Professor. (*Calms down*) Okay, so what do you want?

Chief. I knew you would come to the point.

Professor. (*Thundering*) *What do you want?*

Chief. You don't have to shout. (*Pause*) I have been told that you have this funny idea of running for the senate.

Femi. And what if he does?

Chief. (*Helpfully*) As a long-standing friend, I will tell you that it's a very unhealthy ambition.

Professor. What are you trying to say?

Chief. I mean, funny things happen these days.

Femi. Like?

Chief. Like people falling off buildings. Or sometimes, you are walking in a dark alley, and someone grabs your throat *(grabs one of his henchmen's throats)* and chokes you, chokes you till you die. Or sometimes people are run over by a trailer or even commit suicide. A million and one things can happen to someone with such a lofty ambition.

Professor. *(Calmly)* Chief Yagba, are you threatening me?

Chief. No, no, of course not! On the contrary, I'm being a good friend. You know, *(grinning)* to be forewarned is to be forearmed.

Professor. Get out!

Chief. This is becoming interesting. Wait till the press finds out who the true father of your son is.

Professor. Nice try. Really, does it matter? A century ago, when America had more austere sexual habits, they elected a president who was widely known to have an illegitimate child. As a candidate, Grover Cleveland was mocked with the chant:

> *'Ma, Ma,*
> *Where's my Pa?'*
> *'Gone to the White House,*
> *Ha, Ha, Ha'*

Chief. *(Claps his hands in glee, obviously likes the chant)* See what I mean? You'll be running against the true father of your illegitimate son.

Professor. *(Going right through his speech)* Grover Cleveland won that election, occasioning his supporters' memorable response:

> *'Hurrah for Maria,*
> *Hurrah for the Kid.*
> *We voted Grover,*
> *And we're damn glad we did.'*

Chief. You don't seem to understand …

Professor. The electorate will be more interested in what happened to the kid and the woman, my dear Chief. I just learnt that fathering a child is one thing and being a man before you become a father is another. Now, leave my house!

Chief. *(Waving his hands expansively)* All right, all right! No need to be temperamental. Good-bye for now, but rest assured that I'll be back. *(Exits with his thugs)*

Professor. *(Apprehensively)* Do you think he means it?

Femi. Of course, he does. I warned you. Chief Yagba is not a man to be trifled with.

Professor. *(Cowering)* This senate business doesn't seem to be such a good idea after all.

Femi. Are you backing out?

Professor. *(Shaking)* Look, were you not here? The man threatened to kill me.

Femi. *(Angrily)* You shouldn't let him get away with it!

Professor. Of course, I won't. I'm going to the police.

Femi. That is a good idea. We'll show that thug that we don't scare easily.

Professor. *(Hesitantly)* Femi, you don't seem to understand.

Femi. Understand what?

Professor. I don't think I will run again.

Femi. Come on, Professor, don't tell me you are chickening out.

Professor. Yes, I am. I have a family to think about.

Femi. Don't tell me you are scared. Remember the words of Martin Luther King: 'The ultimate measure of a man is not where he stands in times of comfort and convenience, but where he stands in times of conflict and controversy'.

Professor. (*Sarcastically*) That's why he got himself killed. Look, I've had enough of this politics business. I think I'm much safer in the classroom. (*Exits*)

Femi. (*Shouting after him*) So, where does that leave me *eh*? Where? What of Alhaji? Iya Mulika? I should have known you for what you are, all mouth and no guts. Shit! (*Kicks the chair*)

Jide enters, arm in a sling, followed by Keji.

Keji. Where is Dad going to?

Femi. (*Very depressed*) He has gone to the police station.

Jide. What happened?

Femi. Chief Yagba just left here. Your father thinks he wants to kill him.

Jide. (*Angrily*) That bastard! If I lay my hands on him ...

Femi. That's not all. Professor is withdrawing from the race.

Keji. (*In shock*) What!

Jide. We've got to stop him.

Femi. I don't think you can. Chief scared the living daylights out of him.

Keji. Come on, let's go!

Keji opens the door and comes face-to-face with Vincent Badmus, a Babariga-wearing, soft-spoken, blubbery-lipped toad of a man.

Keji. Hello, can I help you?

Vincent. (*In a drawling American accent*) Hi, I'm Vincent Badmus, the youth leader of the Nigerian Action Party.

Jide. (*Sarcastically*) Hey, everyone! Look what we have here! A baby politician.

Femi. Are you not the son of Chief Erasmus Badmus, the oil billionaire?

Vincent. I sure am. Actually I'm here to solicit your support.

Keji. Go ahead.

Vincent. The youth of our great party have chosen Chief Yagba as our flag bearer at the upcoming senatorial election, and as the youth leader …

Jide. *(Cuts him short)* Wait a minute, as the youth leader? Do I understand it to mean leader of youth like us?

Vincent. *(Confidently)* But of course. I was elected at …

Femi. *(Angrily cuts him short)* Selected!

Vincent. *(Helpfully)* Well, that is 'homegrown democracy' for you. I read something about it the other day. It's called selective election by adoption, SEA for short.

Jide. *(Feigning interest)* Mr. Badmus, where did you receive primary education?

Vincent. You mean grade school?

Jide. *(Angrily)* Whatever you call it.

Vincent. In the United States.

Keji. And your secondary education?

Vincent. Actually, we call it high school. That was in the United States as well.

Femi. And your university education was in the United States too?

Vincent. Actually, I attended college in the United States, Harvard, to be precise.

Jide. That is to say that you never sat for JAMB?

Vincent. Hey, what are you guys driving at?

Jide. Answer this question first. Did you or did you not sit for JAMB?

Vincent. Of course not.

Jide. What sport do you like: football, hockey, volleyball, what sport?

Vincent. I play baseball and American football, though I'm not really good at either.

Jide. There you are. You don't know the agony of waiting for JAMB, you have never played football, *ludo,* or *Ayo* before, and yet you claim to be a Nigerian youth leader. *(Turning to Femi and Keji)* Guys, what should we do with this clown?

Femi and Keji. Kick his ass!

Jide. So, what are we waiting for?

They pursue Vincent out of the house.

Jide. *(Fuming)* Imagine the rascal, to come here claiming to be our leader.

Femi. But that is the real tragedy. Our youth, I mean the real youth, have refused to get involved, leaving politics to thugs and school dropouts. Yet we are always the most vocal when it comes to complaining about the failures of the system.

Keji. A very valid point, Femi. Let us rally behind a candidate of our choice, someone who can understand our frustrations, a real Nigerian youth.

Jide. I get it, Femi. Because you have political ambitions, you want us to rally behind you and vote you in. This is about you, isn't it?

Femi. On the contrary; it is about you. I am nominating you as our leader.

Jide. *(In amazement)* Me! You can't be serious.

Keji. Why not? You have the charisma, the energy, and the aggression. Let's face it: Daddy is too scared to stand the heat of an election with Chief.

Jide. Hey! Slow down; I don't think I can handle this.

Femi. And why not?

Keji. If we work as a team, you can.

Jide. *(Beginning to like the idea).* Hmm. That might work.

Keji. Yeah! That's the spirit.

Femi. So, how do we fund the campaign?

Silence.

Black

Scene IX

Professor and Folake are in the sitting room. Keji enters.

Folake. What's the matter?

Keji. I had a terrible day.

Folake. You don't sound happy. *(Silence)* It's a man, isn't it? Why don't you tell me about it?

Professor. *(Laughing)* The Lady of Shalott. *(Still laughing).* The Lady of Shalott's look.

Keji. Who is the Lady of Shalott?

Professor. *(In amazement)* You mean you did not read Tennyson?

Folake. Who?

Professor. Lord Alfred Tennyson.

Keji. *(Helpfully)* Another literary figure.

Professor. I quote:
> *Out flew the web and floated wide;*
> *The mirror crack'd from side to side;*
> *'The curse is come upon me!' cried*
> *The Lady of Shalott.*

That's the look you had on your face, the Lady of Shalott's look.

Folake. Don't mind your father.

Keji. *(Close to tears)* All men are the same; they use you and dump you.

Folake. *(Holding her; consolingly)* I don't understand young men of these days. You have a good job, earn an astronomical salary, are educated, even have a master's degree. It beats me. You are intelligent, personable, articulate, well read, yet men seem to run away from you.

Keji. *(Angrily)* Men only want one thing. Once they get it, they are out as fast as they came.

Professor. That's not correct. I am still here with your mother.

Keji. You are a special breed.

Professor. Don't you get the point? It is not about me; it's about you.

Keji. Me?

Professor. Yes, you! You are scaring the men off. What you should be asking is, 'What is wrong with me?'

Keji. There is nothing wrong with me.

Professor. Not only you; I'm talking about you and your kind.

Keji. I don't understand.

Professor. Look at you. Your entire personality projects an 'I don't need a man' message, so you end up without one.

Keji. Don't you tell me the kind of image I should project!

Folake. He is right, Keji. The skills that make one successful in her career are not necessarily the skills that make a successful relationship.

Professor. *(Counting off on his fingers)* Linear thinking, multitasking, self-reliance, structured goals, and direct action. Okay, they help you in the boardroom; but my dear, they can't help you in the bedroom.

Keji. *(Aghast)* You mean I should play the dumb village girl because I want to get a man interested in me?

Folake. In this environment, my dear, you may have to stoop to conquer.

Keji. *(Sarcastically)* I see. Being acknowledged as the boss is very important to our menfolk.

Professor. It's not that. Even if a man is attracted to you, he'll discover that you have very little space for him in your life.

Keji. *(Obstinately)* My career is my life. I'm not about to give it up because of one stupid man.

Professor. *(In exasperation)* There she goes again.

Folake. Keji, as it is now, between your career and your ambitions, you are seldom there for any man, much less a stupid one.

Professor. She will be too busy to prepare him a home-cooked meal or to be a listening ear to his problems as she is preoccupied with her own. My dear, by the time you are forty-five, you may wish you had set different priorities while you were younger.

Folake. To be ambitious is good, but my dear, it's so easy to save your career and lose your man.

Keji. So I should recalibrate my priorities—that is what I hear you say?

Professor. Not recalibrate, just realign them with present realities. You are playing men on their own turf, toe-to-toe, neck and neck. Men like women for the ways they are different from them, not the ways they are the same.

Keji. I should bury my ambitions. That is what you are trying to say?

Folake. Keji, a hardworking career woman is good to have in your office; but when a man goes home, he'd prefer a loving partner.

Keji. For Christ's sake, we are not in the stone age! This is the threshold of the twenty-first century.

Professor. Get me right! I did not say that women should be seen and not heard. I actually like ambitious women myself. If not, I wouldn't have married your mother.

Keji. *(Covering her ears)* All right, all right! You two just sit there in all your righteous glory and judge me! Listen! I don't want to be what you want me to be. I want to be me! Okay? Me! And that's good enough! *(Runs upstairs)*

Professor. There she goes again, the Lady of Shalott.

Folake. (*Angrily*) Oh, shut up!

Sounds of a parade are heard from outside—drums, trumpets, and singing. Jide enters dressed in a flowing Babariga. Femi is right behind him, and the noise of singing and cheering is still heard from backstage.

Professor. Hey! What's going on?

Femi. We are here to remind you that the senatorial primaries of our party will take place tomorrow.

Jide. (*Proudly*) The youth wing of our party has with one voice nominated me as our party flag bearer.

Professor. (*In disbelief*) Really! Young man, politics, especially Nigerian politics, is a very expensive venture. How do you intend to fund this project?

Femi. That's all taken care of.

Folake. How?

Jide. Mum, you don't want to know. But trust me, that is why I am the director.

Folake. So, when is the election taking place?

Jide. This time tomorrow.

Keji enters.

Professor. Don't you think you are too young for this? If you must do this at all, don't you think you should wait for the next elections? Then you will have matured, made a name for yourself, built a war chest.

Jide. (*Condescendingly*) Professor, there is no better time for the youth to get involved in the politics of our country than this time. I have decided to quit complaining and commence positive action. I have decided that I will stop demanding change and create change, be the change driver. That is the only way the Nigeria of our dreams will become a reality.

Keji. (*Angrily*) Tell that bastard beside you to get out of here!

Jide. Who? You mean Femi?

Femi. (*Apologetically*) Keji, I'm sorry for the way I behaved today. I didn't mean to make you feel bad.

Professor. You mean Femi was your date?

Folake. (*Angrily*) You sneaky bastard. We give you a roof, give you a job, and your only gratitude is to go after my hapless daughter.

Femi. But I love her!

Professor, Folake, and Jide. *What!*

Femi. I want to marry her.

Jide. (*Angrily*) You are not serious. You can't even feed and fend for yourself, and you want to marry my sister?

Femi. (*Almost pleading*) If you accept me, we'll survive.

Shouts of 'Chief! Chief!' draw their attention. Chief strides in with Alhaji and Iya Mulika in tow.

Jide. (*Angrily*) What are you looking for here?

Chief. (*Bemused*) You are beginning to sound like your true father.

Professor. (*Angrily*) Answer the boy! What do you want?

Chief. I have a business proposition to make. Alhaji, Iya Mulika, you can wait outside.

Folake. (*Angrily*) We have had enough of your tricks. Please leave us alone.

Chief. Actually, it's Femi I want to talk to.

Femi. Me?

Chief. Yes, you. I've had mutually beneficial discussions with Alhaji and Iya Mulika. It appears that we have a lot of things in common.

Jide. (*Unsure*) What are you saying?

Chief. Femi, come and work for me. I'll pay you well.

Femi. (*Angrily*) I thought as much. You just want to insult me before all these good people. Listen up, Mister or Chief or whatever you call yourself, I cannot be bought; I will not sell my conscience!

Chief. (*Cutting through his speech*) Twenty five thousand naira per week.

Femi. Not even for that, not for all the gold in …

Chief. Thirty thousand naira per week.

Femi. I am not moved. I remain solidly by the side of …

Chief. Fifty thousand naira per week.

Femi. (*Capitulating*) The man who can pay my bills. When do I start?

Chief. (*Beaming; clapping his hands in glee*) Excellent. I believe that fifty thousand naira a week is a fair starting salary … (*conspiratorially*) and there are performance bonuses, of course. This is your first paycheque, upfront. (*Hands out the cheque*)

Jide. (*In disappointment*) Femi, you can't do this.

Chief. Let's go, Femi.

Keji. (*Mockingly*) I thought you said you love me?

Femi. (*Stops in his tracks; slight pause*) That was a business proposition. I have a better proposition now.

Professor. (*Shaking his head in disappointment*) You are a disgrace to my late friend. I can't believe you are his son.

Femi. My father was a great politician, but he died a poor man. I will not disgrace him. I'll be a great politician and die a very rich man. Good-bye, Professor, it was a pleasure working for you.

Chief. And you Professor, advise your son, I mean my son, in his own interest to abandon any hope he has of taking up from where you chickened out, or he'll be roasted like a chicken. Let's go!

Exit Chief and Femi. There is a long silence.

Folake. (*Breaking down*) So, where do we go from here?

Keji. Calm down, Mummy, calm down.

Jide. *(Confidently, angrily)* Daddy, I am your son. I don't care whether that thug sired me or not. You have been my father; you are still my father.

Professor. *(Embracing him)* Yes, son, you are my son, and I am your father.

Folake. And I am your mother and your wife. In that capacity, I'm advising both of you to forget this dream of yours. I would never forgive myself if something bad happens to either of you.

Silence as Professor and Jide stare at each other.

Professor. Are you thinking what I'm thinking?

Jide. *(Nodding)* I think I am.

Keji. *(Apprehensive)* What is going on?

Jide. *(With a note of finality)* I am going ahead with the election.

Professor. And I'm solidly behind you.

Folake. *(Pleading)* My dear, politics is a dirty game. You'll be cheated, backstabbed. You might even lose your life in the process. Keji, please talk to them.

Keji. I'm sorry, Mum, I am with them on this one. Chief Yagba and his ilk had better get ready to kill all of us if they think that this time around we will sit complacently, twiddling our toes, while they destroy our country, destroy our future.

Folake. What! *(Slight pause)* Okay. Now that I know that you are all ready to die, I don't plan to be left behind. Jide, when did you say the election is taking place?

Jide. This time tomorrow.

Folake. Then our tomorrow starts today. Let's go. We have an election to win.

Jide. *(Growing in confidence)* That is the very first battle to be won. Then we win the war: we recapture our country from the clutches of Chief Yagba and his cronies.

Professor. *(Grinning and strumming an imaginary guitar)* Dum dum dum dum dum … Well spoken, my son.

Keji. *(Quizzically)* What are you doing?

Professor. *(Laughing, waltzing across the room)* Banishing the strums of depression.

Jide. The strums of what?

Professor. Clearly you have not read the 'Strums of Depression' by Jekwu Ozoemene: *(Light dims, and spotlight focuses on Professor.)*

We grew up riding on Orpheus notes,

Singing along the coast of Coromandel

(Where the early pumpkins grow),

Manning *Hispaniola*'s wheel as we rode the waves

Journeying to the faraway tree,

Conjuring with Hecate and her cohorts as fire burned and cauldron bubbled.

And Narnia! Oh! There was Narnia.

But they have killed Orpheus,

His lyre now played by the dyslexic, stubby fingers of leprous hands,

Rendering mournful strums of depression,

While our mother muse mourns his martyrdom.

They have killed Orpheus,

His death a testimony to our collective neglect,

For we ostracised Nancy Drew, banished the Hardy Boys,

Tarred and feathered Brothers Grimm and ran Hans Andersen out of town.

We let them kill Orpheus,

First asphyxiated by the gun-wielding junta,

Whose bland rhetoric was dwarfed by the flowery poetic language of the gods,

For when they played their martial music,

Orpheus it was who played music more beautiful and louder,

Drowning out the Sirens' bewitching songs.

They have killed Orpheus,

And at his passing, men and gods wept (and still weep),

For no longer do we charm the birds with our lovely songs,

Lure the fish and wild beasts with our feathery oratory,

Coax the trees and rocks to dance.

No longer can our words divert the course of raging rivers,

Our writings lead the destiny of nations, halt advancing armies,

Conquer Hades,

Lure the powerful hounds of hell to sleep,

And give us the audacity of hope.

That is why they killed Orpheus, you know,

For without his depth we are naked,

Bound and gagged by the shackles of ignorance,

Vulnerable captives of the philistine beast

Riding listlessly on these strums of depression.

Jide, Folake, and Keji. Professor!

Professor. You kids should read more, you know. A little education wouldn't hurt you.

Black

THE END

About the Playwright

Nigerian banker, poet, and playwright Jekwu Ozoemene was born in Lagos, Nigeria. He attended Federal Government College Enugu in Nigeria, where his membership in the school's drama club sowed the initial seeds for his romance with the theatre as a playwright and subsequently as a director. He later earned a degree in English from the University of Lagos Akoka-Yaba in Lagos and was a prominent member and coordinator of the foremost theatre group on campus at the time, Theatre 15 Unilag (also known as T15). He went on to obtain a specialist MBA in finance from the University of Leicester in the United Kingdom.

In 2009, Ozoemene published an anthology of poetry in the Editor's Choice–winning book *Shadows of Existence: An Anthology of Poetry. The Anger of Unfulfillment—Three Plays Out of Nigeria* is his first collection of plays; all three plays in this collection, have been staged in the past.

He currently lives in Port Harcourt, Nigeria, with his wife and two young children. He enjoys reading, running, going to the movies, watching stage plays, exercising, and facilitating youth mentoring programs. He also teaches project and real estate finance at the Financial Institutions Training Centre (FITC) in Lagos.